Alternatives in Education

PETER LANG
New York • Washington, D.C./Baltimore • Boston • Bern
Frankfurt am Main • Berlin • Brussels • Vienna • Canterbury

Greg S. Goodman

Alternatives
in Education

Critical Pedagogy
for Disaffected
Youth

PETER LANG
New York • Washington, D.C./Baltimore • Boston • Bern
Frankfurt am Main • Berlin • Brussels • Vienna • Canterbury

Library of Congress Cataloging-in-Publication Data

Goodman, Greg S.
Alternatives in education: critical pedagogy
for disaffected youth / Greg S. Goodman.
p. cm.
Includes bibliographical references and index.
1. Alternative education—United States—Case studies. 2. Alternative
schools—United States—Case studies. 3. Critical pedagogy—
United States—Case studies. 4. Problem youth—
Education—United States—Case Studies. I. Title.
LC46.4.G66   371.04'0973—dc21   98-53166
ISBN 0-8204-4430-8

Die Deutsche Bibliothek-CIP-Einheitsaufnahme

Goodman, Greg S.:
Alternatives in education: critical pedagogy
for disaffected youth / Greg S. Goodman.
–New York; Washington, D.C./Baltimore; Boston; Bern;
Frankfurt am Main; Berlin; Brussels; Vienna; Canterbury: Lang.
ISBN 0-8204-4430-8

Cover design by James F. Brisson

The paper in this book meets the guidelines for permanence and durability
of the Committee on Production Guidelines for Book Longevity
of the Council of Library Resources.

Printed in the United States of America

To Peter Ordway and Barbara Carlson
for appreciating and encouraging the maverick in me.

TABLE OF CONTENTS

viii

The priorities in our society are out of whack. Educators are paid less than prison guards, we are building correctional institutions as fast as possible, and there are constant calls for excellence and standards for students in our schools that are unrealistic for the majority of our students. Many educators discuss the changes that need to occur within our schools, but the "doing it" is much more elusive and few books actually provide specifics about how to make real change. However, Greg Goodman has done exactly that.

I have had the wonderful experience of being involved in this endeavor since Greg first mentioned he wanted to write a book about alternative education. I myself have worked for several years in the juvenile justice system and Greg and I had, on many occasions, discussed the problems facing the students with whom we worked. His devotion to these students has always been obvious and the means by which to not only educate them but truly care for them has been his passion.

Such students need educators like Greg. They need educators who are willing to go the "extra mile," and do what others have not previously done, whether due to lack of knowledge or lack of understanding. They need educators and the other adults who are able to recall their own adolescent days in order to have some inkling of what the at-risk student is experiencing. Finally, these students need educators who are sensitive to their dress, their language, their music, and, most importantly, their self-esteem.

Greg has written a book that is funny, sad, and at times scary about the realities of working with alternative education students. But more than simply relate his experiences he provides the reader with the methods and ideas that *work* with these students. To ignore this book is to ignore these students.

I know you will have as much fun reading this book as I did. Then go out there and make a difference for these complex, difficult young people who have something positive to give to our communities.

Karen T. Carey
Fresno, California
January 1999

There are many arenas where critical educators work to make a difference for our youth. Some work at the level of policy, fighting in and against state legislatures and local school boards for those necessary changes that will level the playing field. Others work with verve and vision in the classrooms of our nation, struggling on a day-to-day basis to make classrooms into vital sites for social transformation and critical citizenship. Still others, and I would include myself in this category, function as cultural workers in universities and other sites, developing both global and local critiques of schooling, and forging counterhegemonic strategies for collective struggle against the depredations of capitalist social relations. None of us work alone. We find the places where we can effect the most change and make our stand. Greg Goodman has chosen the classroom where he has worked for twenty-five years as a counselor-educator. And now he has expanded the horizon of his critical work by writing a book and sharing his hard-won lessons with those readers lucky enough to read through these pages. Greg has written a book about the struggle to reframe our schools and to reinvent them as democratic institutions. In doing so he has drawn upon some of the insights from those of us who work in different arenas—such as critical pedagogy and cultural studies—and he has shared with us how these approaches can provide students in alternative education with rich and invigorating experiences. He has also drawn upon some time-tested approaches that he has carried with him for decades, such as experiential learning and approaches that address the psychological and social needs of disaffected and alienated youth who have been abused and infantilized by our market culture.

Greg Goodman knows a great deal about creating alternative approaches to education through democratizing the experience and learning of students and I am pleased that teachers now have the opportunity to share Greg's expertise and his passion for social justice.

Peter McLaren
Los Angeles, California
March 1999

ACKNOWLEDGMENTS

I wish to thank some of the many people who contributed to the evolution of this book. Karen Carey deserves tremendous credit for providing many insightful readings and constant encouragement. Her tireless efforts buoyed me in times of doubt. Jim Jelmberg loaned the concept of relentless focus. Dwight Webb shared unconditional strokes. Ray Scannell provided an alternative education practitioner's unique perspective. David Swain saw the potential from the psychologist's eye. Ken Grossman, the former director of the Alt, kept me honest. Binbin Jiang contributed a Chinese multicultural reading. Susan Goodman's determination demonstrated to me that the process of writing a book is a long, yet possible, proposition. Robert DeVillar tossed in some seasoned authorial suggestions. Barbara Morton has been the trusted editor and a believer in the book's possibility.

The book's final hurdle was conquered with the support of Peter McLaren and James Fraser. Their appreciation of the book's value as a resource for alternative educators and others in the field of education gave the book the validation necessary to gain the notice of Peter Lang. McLaren's presence is ubiquitous in the world of critical theory, and his voice is resonant in this text!

Finally, I wish to thank all of the teachers who helped me in my growth as a person and who appreciated my struggle with the traditional approach to teaching and learning. Foremost on that list is Paul Brockelman. And to my wife, Andrea, for helping me every day with her smile and support. For these people and the relationships we sustain, I offer my most heartfelt appreciation.

> I found that my memories of school helped me to avoid doing hateful things to my pupils that my teachers had done to me. (Kohl, 1969, p. 70)

My interest in alternative education methodologies formally began nearly thirty years ago at the University of New Hampshire (UNH). While the country was embroiled in the Vietnam War, universities were enmeshed in a challenge to traditional approaches to the process of teaching and learning. Leading the charge in the philosophy department at UNH was a courageous maverick named Paul Brockelman. Paul was a theologian. As would befit his background in theology, he was a masterful craftsman of sermonlike lectures for educational change. I would sit mesmerized by his lectures. Most memorable to me was his talk on hope and despair. Much of the despair that I felt and the depression that I experienced Paul could trace to the lifeless and pedantic styles of instruction that I had often experienced in school.

When I think back to my earliest school days, I can remember the first experience of loss of joy at school. My first-grade teacher, Miss Bunker, was the sort of woman who would instill fear in her students as a method of control. She could identify students and humiliate them in a second as she continued her reign on the five- and six-year-olds under her command. My first day in her class, I embarrassed myself with an overt expression of joy that was clearly inappropriate for a first-grader in her classroom. Coming from another school where the ringing of the school bell meant, "You are free to go to recess," I leapt up from my chair on the first ring. Skipping merrily down my aisle toward the class exit, I suddenly became aware of the glare of Miss Bunker's eye. All of my classmates were still seated, and I was embarrassed that I alone was up and skipping about. In stark contrast to the order imposed by Miss Bunker, this act was tantamount to revolution. My consequence was that I was made to stay in from recess and counseled never to act so impetuously ever again. Little did we both know that this insurrection was to be the beginning of a long and painful thirteen years of "educating" this author!

By the time I completed high school, my personal educational odyssey was replete with reprimands, suspensions and, finally, an expulsion from a then aspiring to be prestigious private school called Derryfield. To make matters worse, high school was a five-year project that spanned three institutions! It is of no little coincidence that I am drawn to the plight of the disaffected. When I heard Paul Brockelman speak about the intellectual arguments for restructuring the teaching and learning process, I found an ally in my quest to more fully understand my frustrations with traditional approaches to education.

Further along my professional and educational path as a school counselor, I was fortunate to be able to hear Rollo May speak about the "Wounded Healer" during the 1985 American Association of Counseling and Development's annual meeting in Houston, Texas. Using metaphors with craft and precision, Rollo May spoke of the healers' (counselors, psychiatrists, and psychologists) desires to help themselves through the process of healing another's wounds. I could relate to May's thesis. My pursuit of a Masters in Counseling and my career in education was an attempt to learn more about my own wounds and to recover from the pains of past mistakes.

This story of how I became interested in alternative education would not be complete without the mention of one of my closest friends and lifelong mentors, Dwight Webb. Dwight was the man who showed me the path through graduate school and the one who has always had faith in my purpose to promote changes in our systems. Dwight taught me the value of singing, playing, and enjoying each day as the gift it can be! Dwight's scholarship of the sensuous gave me hope that there were others that shared my contempt for the staid. Dwight rejoiced in his ability to help others find their spot and purpose on the planet. With Dwight's help, I was able to connect myself to a career that has included passing the hope along to hundreds of children and their parents. My desire for this book is to share my learnings of what works best with the students that traditional approaches have failed.

The needs of today's youth parallel the needs of youth past, but the stakes, in terms of consequences, greatly exceed those of yesterday. The methamphetamine drugs; suicide; terminal, sexually transmitted diseases; youth gang violence; and other atrocities today's youth face dwarf the old teenage issues. Whereas it was a rarity to hear of a young person being incarcerated forty years ago, today the juvenile facilities are one of the country's largest industries. Before we drown in our own ignorance of how to educate and rehabilitate our youth, we need to learn how we can help these students become productive citizens in tomorrow's society. Our other choice, continuing to exclude or lock up every miscreant, will bankrupt our country both financially and spiritually.

This book is about why and how we can change our educational institutions for our students of today. The book's process has evolved through my doctoral studies in the Joint Doctoral Program in Educational Leadership with the Fresno State University and University of California (UCLA and Davis) faculties. The content of the text is derived from my graduate studies and twenty-five years of work as a counselor-educator. For the completion of this book, I am particularly grateful for the inspiration, guidance, and hard work of Dr. Karen Carey. Her encouragement of my writing has helped me bridge many of the inevitable resistant periods in this book's evolution.

NOTE: All of the names in this book have been changed to protect the anonymity of the individuals involved in the Alt. The protection of confidentiality that the Alt included within its rules continues throughout the publication of this text.

CHAPTER 1

A Rationale for Alternative Education

Although society is being dramatically altered, schools appear to be changing little if at all. (Pianta and Walsh, 1996, p. 96)

During the past twenty-five years in my work as a school psychologist and as an educator, I have witnessed many children and their families as they engaged in a struggle with schooling. The struggles all bear the unique stamp of the individuals that experienced the expulsion, suspension, or other form of rejection; yet the individuals are bonded together in their alienation and elimination from further participation in the schooling process. These students sometimes evoke educators' tears of frustration, but, more often, their behavior evokes a rage that leaves the student ostracized from the school. Their misbehavior, be it prankish or criminal, is challenging us to question our professional skills and our ethics.

This book looks at systematic and methodological techniques that work to address the needs of disaffected youth. I have combined personal experience and research to craft a methodology that can help to keep kids in school and to show them that our society needs them to succeed. Many important educational paradigms have evolved during the past twenty years. Advances in psychology and psychosocial theory have contributed greatly to our ability to understand, and often to ameliorate, the problems of today's youth. The question remains, how will we carry out the job of reaching the kids we've become accustomed to excluding?

We need to commit ourselves to the task of providing success for all students if we are going to build a just community. A school's miscreants are dealt with one by one. Student suspensions and expulsions are generally handled individually. In the race to complete the paperwork and facilitate the process, administrators rarely have the time to examine what is the total effect of this process of exclusion. These individual students comprise approximately twenty-five percent of our nation's school population. In the inner city, failure rates loom near the fifty percent mark! This book seeks to examine the needs of disaffected youth from a psychologist's perspective. Self-esteem for disaffected youth is the central issue. Knowledge of successful techniques is the tool that can help us provide effective programs to teach these most challenging students.

As we attempt to better understand the plight of our nation's at-risk youth, there is much to gain from an examination of the educational process as it has occurred in California. California is the Mecca of diversity; it is quickly approaching the time when its schools will be forty-eight percent Hispanic and twenty-five percent Caucasian (Munitz, 1995). Ethnographic changes are but one of the many aspects of California's demography that affect schools and communities. High rates of attrition (thirty-six percent according to the California Department of Education), and the impact of social problems, such as unemployment and poverty, are causing considerable conflict on campuses and within communities throughout California (Wirt and Kirst, 1992). These demographics are instructive when they are compared to the other large states such as Texas, New York, and Michigan (Pianta and Walsh, 1996). In these richly diverse school districts many minority population students experience high rates of exclusion. Problems within our education system are, in fact, widespread and in need of remediation. I would add that these problems exist not only in the United States, but also throughout North America (Ministry of Education Annual Report, 1994–95).

This is not to say that there have not been efforts to change the system to accommodate at-risk youth. An examination of California's efforts to meet the needs of these students provides insight into the evolution of our attempts to deal with disaffected youth all across the nation. The general trend in California has been to identify and remove the miscreants and troublemakers. Using educational statutes related to misbehavior, school authorities have placed students in alternative programs ranging from independent study to continuation schools. Some students have been expelled entirely. Laws such as the California Gun-Free Schools Act specifically require the expulsion of any student caught in possession of a firearm on a school campus. Although no one would argue with the premise that school is not the place for a firearm, especially in the wake of the tragic events that we witness across our nation, I question the wisdom of further alienating the students who do not fit by removing them from the possibility of further or alternative education.

Unfortunately, many alternative programs that our former regular education students attend are strikingly similar to the program that the student was unsuccessful in to begin with. As Wirt and Kirst (1992) have noted, our educational system tends to change by addition. We believe that our original direction, or model, is correct. We then modify the model by adding on bits to the initial framework. In this way, we create programs either within existing schools or on other campuses that often look just like the programs that were not working with these students in the beginning. Because we continue to fail so many of our future citizens by not placing them in educational programs that work, we perpetuate the alienation that placed these students in risk categories such as a discontinuous and unsuccessful school experience! To change the cycle of failure for these students, we need to develop and foster alternative models to reach these potential school leavers.

One of the unfortunate consequences of the failure of schools to retain students and educate them for a productive role in society is the growth of the juvenile justice system and its various constituencies. The correlation between school failure and poor performance in society is all too clear. Ninety-eight percent of all of the juveniles that were incarcerated in 1993 were high school dropouts (Ingersoll and LeBoeuf, 1997). As the criminal justice system continues to overwhelm our society with its insatiable growth, it is instructive to trace that system to its start to further our understanding of why the educational and social systems need to change.

The history of attempts to constructively deal with disaffected California youth dates back to the founding of the first industrial school on May 5, 1859. However, it wasn't until 1891 that the first reformatory was opened. This facility served 300 boys and girls. Fifty years later the California Youth Authority (CYA) was established (1941) to assist the state in meeting the needs of 1,080 wards in three institutions. CYA now houses nearly 10,000 inmates and oversees 6,000 parolees (Wedge, 1995).

Because of our school's failures, the needs of our society for a new way to teach at-risk youth could not be greater, nor more obvious, than they are today (Orfield, 1988). California leads the nation; nearly 10,000 youth (9,717 in 1993) live within its eleven institutions and four youth detention camps (Wedge, 1995). Thousands more are living in group homes and treatment programs that are attempting to help them recover from a multiplicity of abuses. Thousands more who are still at home are enrolled in independent study. These are the students who have been ostracized from the mainstream because of violent behavior, suicidal ideation, pregnancy, drug abuse, or any of the violations of California Education Code 48900 that may result in removal from its educational system based upon the philosophy of zero tolerance. Increasingly, our society is attempting to exclude the perpetrators of crime and disruption. Removal from comprehensive high schools for the safety of other students is rational (Carey, 1996). However, it is clear that ostracizing these youths is not reversing the trends that are contributing to these overwhelming statistics.

What the statistics do indicate is that approximately one third of the school leavers enter the criminal justice system (Cairns and Cairns, 1994). It is apparent that a person with no education or marketable skills is at a disadvantage when they look for meaningful employment within our communities. Consequently, these individuals are finding themselves connected to a lifestyle that is countercultural or criminal (McCall, 1994). It is becoming more apparent to our society that turning ill-prepared youth out of school and onto the streets is a prescription for failure, if not for delinquency. Sadly, the national response is to dispose of these people in prison with the result that the possibility that they will be included decreases and they are further alienated from the community.

How these societal failures end up is well documented. Ingersoll and LeBoeuf found that a 1995 report from the National Office of Juvenile Justice and Delinquency Prevention stated that "seventeen percent of youth entering prison had not completed grade school (eighth grade or less). One fourth had completed tenth grade, and two percent had completed high school or possessed a GED degree" (Ingersoll and LeBoeuf, 1997, p. 2). Fortunately, not all school leavers end up in jail, but of the jail inhabitants, the majority are school dropouts. Given the huge numbers of school leavers, the cost to society of incarcerating these miscreants is staggering. Furthermore, school dropouts lack the skills, training, and perseverance necessary to find gainful employment in our economy. With an attrition rate of thirty-six percent, the failure on the part of the schools to retain more students appears to be epidemic!

The daily newspapers document the increased stresses that affect young people. Examples abound of gang violence (Vigil, 1988), teenage pregnancy, teen suicides, drug abuse, and high dropout rates (Kozol, 1982). Clearly, the solution of the eighties and even today, that is, zero tolerance, does not reverse or even slow the demographic changes that are so disastrous to the future of our society. Even more alarming is the forecast for the future. Reporter Andy Furillo of the *Sacramento Bee* writes that "the California Youth Authority's population is projected to grow by 28% over the next five years" (Furillo, 1995). This does not include the thousands currently on parole, the 124,000 plus youth annually admitted to juvenile hall, or the 250,000 arrests that preceded those detainments (Wedge, 1994). Will these numbers grow by twenty-eight percent also?

The traditional family has suffered the demographic changes to a greater degree than any other social unit. In 1997, thirty-three percent of the children born in California were born out of wedlock and 70,000 of those children were born to teenagers (Markert, 1997). Nationally, over half of all families have single parents or are "reconstituted" (that is, they include stepparents). Many of these families have experienced a negative financial impact through the divorce process. Because most families require two breadwinners for survival, life on one income often means a move into an apartment, or, to some, homelessness. The resulting feelings that children have of anger, loss, and hurt often are precursors to a lack of resiliency and, concomitantly, to school failure.

And what of the thousands that successfully commit suicide? These are the students who turn their rage inward. The numbers, curiously enough, are roughly parallel to the incarceration rates. The number of juvenile hall residents who were later incarcerated in adult facilities in 1992 was 23 youths for every 10,000 in the hall (Wedge, 1994). Suicide attempts approximate 15 of every 10,000 youths. Successful suicides number 1.2 per 10,000 (Page, 1996). These are certainly not numbers that reinforce the notion that our society is doing a good job with the at-risk group of our nation's youth.

How shall we define "at-risk"? Growing up in the turn of this second millennium could well be construed to be risky for everyone.

All families have the potential to undergo an experience that could put children at-risk. However, the majority of our youth are successful even when they experience stress that put them at risk. This ability to be resilient to at-risk factors is the key to a healthy lifestyle and to success in society (Peng, 1994). In many ways, using the label "at-risk" or any other label (such as disaffected) is not productive. Labeling can contribute to the perpetuation of the problem rather than to its solution. Throughout this book, the use of the terms at-risk and disaffected are meant to *describe* school leavers, not to diagnose or to label them.

We are looking to one another for help, because we have learned that no single agency is capable of tackling these societal problems on their own. School personnel often contend that they are in the business of education, not rehabilitation. Community mental health agencies view the breakdown of the family as a societal problem too large for mental health professionals to fix (Hillman, 1996). The criminal justice system can't launch proactive programs beyond Drug and Alcohol Refusal Education (DARE) because the majority of its resources are committed to law enforcement. To improve our society's chances of reversing the negative impact of school failure, we need to change the way we deliver programs for at-risk youth and all the youth agency players need to cooperate as partners (Edwards, 1996). Working through an interagency task force (Fontana and Martinez, 1997) approach, some communities are trying to unite the powers that provide youth services in order to develop better ways of serving at-risk youth. Solving the problems of today requires all members of society to join together to seek solutions to the multifaceted problems we face. We are a nation, not at risk (National Commission on Excellence in Education, 1983); we are a nation at war with ourselves. Our youth are killing each other and themselves. It is time for some new answers to the question: "What can we do?"

The History and Future of Options in Education

Much of which has been said so far is borrowed from what Plato
first consciously taught the world. (Dewey, 1916, p. 88)

As education has evolved from the time of Socrates to today, it may
seem that the only remaining constant in the process is the lone
learner. Although many educational historians chastise education for
remaining stuck in a mire of pedagogy centered on teachers and
subjects, the fact that the process has changed is too compelling to
ignore. Education has changed from membership in an elite, private
club to a more egalitarian and pluralistic experience. Further,
changes in the demographic makeup of our schools, broad economic
support, technological innovations, continual doubling of our
collective knowledge, and advances in practically every aspect of the
educational process have brought about major improvements for the
lives of today's students and teachers.

There have also been major shifts in public educational ideology
in the last one hundred years. During the early part of the nineteenth
century, the ideas of Horace Mann led the country to achieve a more
democratic distribution of free, public education for all. This
systemization of instruction provided the establishment of a wholesale public education practice all across America. The industriali-
zation of the United States coupled with the moral and economic
arguments for removing children from the factories demanded a
system of compulsory education. In many ways the schools replaced
the factories as the warehouses of the youth of the country. The
purposes of the public school system were to prepare future citizens
to establish their rightful place in the U.S. labor market. High
achievers netted high-status college and club acceptance. Low
achievers took the tailings.

It was not until Dewey that the public was to hear a significant
voice of dissent regarding revision of this mass-production method
of education (Dewey, 1916). Dewey reminded Americans that the
purpose of education was to encourage the development of free and
independent thinkers to live in a democratic society. This emphasis

upon the individual was in contrast to the impersonal, industrial mentality that dominated the country. The progressive and humanistic notions of Dewey won the hearts of a small, liberal following. However, the majority of Americans continued to support traditional Socratic and eighteenth-century German hierarchical models. Schools as channeling agents for the growing, capitalistic society seemed more aligned with the continuing hope of fulfilling the American dream.

Although Dewey's work was slow to gain acceptance, during the last three decades there has been a growing movement away from the traditional, uniform, and wholesale "democratizing" of the masses (Raywid, 1995). As we have evolved from an industrial power to a knowledge-driven, postmodern society, the demand for free choice and expanded services has contributed to the development of many more options for students. We now must have an educated populace. It is no longer possible for adults to support themselves or their family without an education or a marketable skill, whereas in the first half of the twentieth century, it was possible to support a family as a laborer. But today's world requires higher levels of skill and knowledge to earn an honest living.

Two of the best examples of major structural changes are the passing of Public Law 94–142, which created the field of special education and laws relating to the guarantee of a free and appropriate public school education such as the Civil Rights Act of 1964. These two laws have greatly expanded the scope of the mandate of education. The effect has been to include thousands of students in programs that enable them to succeed in school.

In addition to the goals of Public Law 94–142 and the emerging civil rights movement, one of the most significant and modern symbols that mark change in education has been the arrival and growth of the alternative or continuation schools. Beginning with the progressive movement that was inspired by John Dewey, the alternative school movement took intellectual form. However, it was not until the late 1960s and early 1970s that alternative schools began to gain acceptance (Young, 1990) and to achieve a widespread physical presence in the educational scene. Mary Anne Raywid (1995), one of alternative education's foremost researchers, traces the term "alternative" to the 1960s when the first alternative schools began to appear within public school systems. Also symbolic of the growth of this movement was the occurrence of the first national alternative schools conference in 1970.

Currently there are over ten thousand alternative schools throughout the country (Young, 1990). These schools are working, each in their own unique way, to try to meet the needs of the millions of students who have found their way out of the traditional program and into the local alternative school. To the credit of the millions of dedicated and professional educators who serve the majority of students in America, regular education does create climates for student success. I believe that in most instances the efforts and intentions of regular education teachers and administrators are well meaning and soundly based in a credible pedagogy. But for those students who do not fit, alternative education can provide viable opportunities (Raywid, 1995). This is especially true if the application of critical pedagogy (Giroux, Lankshear, McLaren, and Peters, 1996; McLaren, 1994) is included in the alternative school's process.

The growth of the alternative school movement has inspired much literature in support of the art and process of alternative schooling (Chalker, 1996; Kellmayer, 1995; Kozol, 1982; Young, 1990). Choice in education is finally emerging on the educational landscape, and it is gaining momentum (Washington State Department of Education, 1995–96). Perceived as a way to ameliorate dissatisfactions with traditional or regular education, alternative education experiences range from individual home schooling of children (Jeub, 1995) to charter schools. In more extreme cases of disenchantment with the operation of the local public schools, some communities have enlisted the support of private entities to run their schools (Sawicky, 1997). For example, the entire school system in Chelsea, Massachusetts, was contracted to be operated by Boston University from 1989 through 1999.

Aligned with the principle of democratic, free choice, Gary Hart's charter schools have inspired a movement to help individuals retake control of their local schools by designing their own (Bierlein and Mulholland, 1994). Charter schools are entities that are established by local citizens to be operated as independent of the public school system. This initiative stems from deep frustrations with systems that continue to operate despite heavy criticism from local groups that feel powerless to effect changes in staff, administration, or curriculum. According to Sawicky (1997), "...a sustained indifference to public dissatisfaction could lead to desperate efforts by parents to break out of the public system through vouchers, home schooling, and other things that dismember public education, root and branch" (p. 32).

The country is alive with home schooling groups and organizations of every type that promote effective options for those who are either left out or thrown out of the local public school. More and more, parents are pulling their students from the public schools and placing them in alternative institutions. For some parents, the choice of sending their student to a private school is made out of religious conviction or, perhaps, family tradition. But in other cases, individuals are suing their local educational agencies and winning private school tuition because the school could not provide the services they are legally mandated to support: a free and appropriate public school education for all their students. In some cases, the school may need to include within its purview the educational needs of a severely emotionally disturbed young person. In the case of a school district with which I am familiar, the school board was obligated to pay a $140,000 annual tuition for an emotionally disturbed student who required residential care. Unfortunately for this school district, the situation took several years to resolve. All the while, the school district bore the financial responsibility.

In light of the needs to provide educational services to an increasingly diverse and demanding public, it behooves local districts to follow the progressive and enlightened example of the state of Washington, which has nearly 200 public schools. Almost all students and their families can find an alternative school that meets their needs. Freedom of choice continues to be a major issue in the educational process. Parents and students need to feel that there is an alternative choice. From that choice, a truly democratic educational system can be fostered. As the handbook and directory of alternative education, *Educational Options and Alternatives in Washington State* (Billings, 1995), states: "Experiential learning, off-campus course work, learning contracts, democratic decision making, new learning environments, restructuring of time, outcome-based credit, parental involvement, project based learning, sensitivity to diverse learning styles, process-focused curriculum, and small size are just a few of the features that have long characterized alternative schools in Washington" (p. 1).

Although many enlightened educators have embraced the notion of alternative education, many other of our political and educational leaders are regressing in their thinking about ways to ameliorate school failure. President Clinton's 1998 State of the Union address called for a national initiative to reinstate grade retention as one of the best choices to help children learn and succeed in school. Although educators can make it appear that students are able to benefit from retention by manipulating the purported outcome of staying back with exaggerations of scholastic accomplishments, any enlightened educator knows that the mismatch of students and schooling is not corrected by more of the same. Lawrence Lieberman (1986) states:

> Some students match up very badly with junior or senior high schools as they exist. These students will never be successful. For them, non-promotion is an evil idea that compounds the original sin of making them go to a standard junior/senior high school in the first place. Some students are not promoted continuously and may remain in the same grade for as much as three or four years. This creates a misery that can only come back and haunt a community. The ripple effect of attitudes developed about schools and education may have far reaching consequences. Rectifying a bad match that has potential disastrous results for both the student and society requires a commitment to alternative schooling. Ultimately, what is called into question is the community's willingness to commit to a view that alternatives are needed for some students and that they will cost money. What is unaffordable is the cost of not providing alternatives. (p. 45)

As we review our options for the twenty-first century, it is important to examine the contributions of our best critical educators and to make more enlightened decisions for our students. There is a match between the theorists of modern pedagogy and the needs of today's youth. As the educational advocates for our students, we need to listen to these voices. To reverse the atrocious rates of attrition (thirty-six percent overall in California in 1994–95), our schools need to embrace a more critical and credible philosophy (see Figure 1).

Figure 1: California Department of Education
Rates of Attrition vs. Rates of Graduation, 1994–95

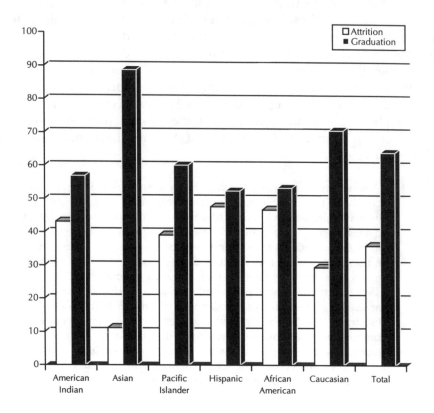

A Philosophy of Alternative Education

> The ignorant man is not the unlearned, but he who does not know himself, and the learned man is stupid when he relies on books, on knowledge and on authority to give him understanding. Understanding comes only through self-knowledge, which is awareness of one's total psychological process. Thus education, in the true sense, is the understanding of oneself, for it is within each one of us that the whole of existence is gathered. (Krishnamurti, 1953, p. 17)

At-risk youth require an atmosphere that acknowledges their essential and unique needs for safety, trust, and recovery from many years of failure (Baker, Bridger, Terry, and Winsor, 1997). Because of these needs, a philosophy for alternative education must be well founded in psychological theory and supported with sound educational practice (Rogers, 1969; Pianta and Walsh, 1996). A philosophy of alternative education is distinguished from traditional educational philosophy in many important ways. The primary difference is the emphasis on psychological components such as individual and interpersonal growth as a precondition for the development of intellect and the enhancement of traditional goals of learning such as reading (Kohl, 1994).

It is instructive to examine the differences between the philosophy of the alternative school movement and the philosophy of the traditional epistemological approach. Traditional pedagogy posits the school's mission as an academically driven, or subject-centered, process. This fact is apparent from the structure of the daily schedule to the reliance on standardized testing to evaluate outcomes. Traditional schools sometimes support the emotional wellness of the students with psychological components, such as the pretense of a guidance counselor. However, the goals of guidance are to further the academic success of students, not supplant academics with therapeutic or psychologically motivated interventions.

I contend that epistemological philosophy fails the needs of at-risk youth and reinforces their exclusion by underacknowledging their psychological requirements. This mismatch between the school's purpose and the needs of at-risk youth is a form of cultural reproduction (Bourdieu, 1977). Cultural reproduction theory states that groups or social classes tend to develop systems that reinforce the power and position that those groups hold. In the case of schools, success is marked by grades and advanced placement. These successes are the product of having the cultural capital to succeed within that system (Bourdieu, 1977). Examples of cultural capital are homework, vocabulary, and personal experience. According to McLaren (1994), "Schools systematically devalue the cultural capital of students who occupy subordinate class positions" (p. 198). I would suggest that a pervasive absence of hope of future success is also a part of the equation. A student without the tools for success, for example, a strong and supportive family, is at a disadvantage. In cultural reproduction theory, such students are already marked to repeat the failing from which they came. Again, according to McLaren (1994), "The end result is that the school's academic credentials remain indissolubly linked to an unjust system of trading in cultural capital which is eventually transformed into economic capital, as working-class students become less likely to get high-paying jobs" (p. 198). The net effect of an epistemological approach upon disaffected students is, simply, an ever-growing group of school dropouts.

Philosophically, the pedagogy for at-risk youth must be fundamentally different than the epistemological foundation of regular education. Alternative schools need to work in a holistic fashion to incorporate the best practices of mental health, education, and systems thinking to build programs that address the needs of the youth they serve (Pianta and Walsh, 1996). This methodology is stated well by Altenbaugh, Engel, and Martin (1995) in their study of Pittsburgh's "school leavers." They state:

> Simplistic solutions, therefore, will only change the form of schooling, but not the substance and structure. Solutions must be comprehensive, acknowledging the complexities of the school leaving process. They must transcend the limits of the existing paradigm of public schooling, and seek creative and flexible approaches, overlooking nothing. All of this must begin with an atmosphere of caring and sensitivity. (p. 155)

It is paramount that the alternative school philosophy reflect a deep understanding of the needs of the student and his or her family as a system of human resources (Pianta and Walsh, 1996). For this reason alternative education philosophy is best structured so that it is primarily psychosocial in nature. This relates to the philosophic paradigms of existentialism and phenomenology. The focus is upon the individual and his or her development as an authentic self. To that end, all of the processes of the school need to reflect a positive valuing of the student and his or her culture. In daily instruction, emphasis needs to remain on the dignity and respect of the student and his or her family.

This aspect of the new alternative school helps to build a positive relationship between the student, their family, and the school personnel. This relationship is fundamental in demonstrating the school's desire to include in an educational experience those who have previously known exclusion (Comer, 1988). Inclusion begins with a psychological process to develop a self-esteem that allows growth and learning. Joy Zimmerman, rephrasing the work of Bonnie Benard, says this well: "Essentially...all youngsters can thrive despite otherwise risky environments if in some area—home, school or the community—a child feels loved and supported; is the object of high expectations; and is given the opportunity to participate and contribute in meaningful ways to the world" (Zimmerman, 1994, p. 3).

The foundation for the success of alternative education students is clearly rooted in their ability to see themselves as lovable and capable individuals (Harris, 1969). It is from a foundation of acceptance of individuals and their cultures that a successful relationship with school and society can be built (Baker, Bridger, Terry, and Winsor, 1997).

To achieve success with at-risk youth, it is paramount that they have a close and personal relationship with their teacher (Kohl, 1994). It is from the relationship with the teacher that alternative education students then develop a personal reason to learn. This relationship is very similar to the relationship that one develops with a mentor. In order to reach and teach these students, the teacher needs to recognize and remember that the influences that lead to the patterns of failure are deeply imbedded in the habitus of that student (MacLeod, 1995).

Jay MacLeod eloquently describes the role of habitus and social reproduction theory in his ethnography of disaffected youth in a Massachusetts housing project. MacLeod (1995) states, "Put simply, the habitus is composed of the attitudes, beliefs, and experiences of those inhabiting one's social world. This conglomeration of deeply internalized values defines an individual's attitudes toward, for example, schooling" (p. 15). From this habitus, there tends to be a reproduction of values over time. Although not all poor and delinquent youth perpetuate habitus characteristics among themselves, the large majority continue the "traditions" set by older siblings, parents, and close friends. Those who break away from those values provide the exceptions to the rules of social reproduction.

In order to break the chains of habitus and to develop routines that foster success in school, a major paradigm shift needs to occur within the alternative education student. For teachers to gain the trust of at-risk youth, the students must first abandon their old connections and belief systems (habitus) before they can learn new ones.

Learning follows the development of safety and trust (Maslow, 1968). One's locus of safety and trust is where the learning is taking place (Hart, 1983). The need for the development of trust is especially strong for minority at-risk learners. According to Ogbu (1995), "Because they do not trust the schools, many minority parents and adults in the community are skeptical that the schools can provide their children with good educations" (p. 98). The cultural capital or set of knowledge and experience that frames one's culture must be respected in order to build a bridge from their culture to that of the school (MacLeod, 1995).

This notion is exemplified by the current debate within the African American community regarding Ebonics (Applebome, 1997). To teach in Oakland, California, a teacher needs to understand and respect the cultural connections that the students possess. By only valuing "white" English, there is an implication of an informal sanction (McLaren, 1994) or rejection of the African American culture. Hispanics and other cultural groups experience this alienation as well. Often the alienation is subtly represented through the null curriculum that leaves out or largely ignores the cultural contributions of minority cultures (Posner, 1995).

The impact of disregarding the student's cultural capital (Bourdieu, 1977) is the subject of a recent research study by the California School Climate and Safety Survey (Bates, Chung, and

Chase, 1996). This work revealed that approximately forty percent of the students in the sample disclosed low levels of trust in their school. In the case of at-risk students, the failure to address their pain and alienation leaves the traditional school unable to reach these potential learners.

Alternative educational philosophy embraces the needs of the individual in their quest for self-knowledge and acceptance (Kozol, 1982). It is only from that place of internal peace or congruence that we will produce a citizen who is prepared to participate in a democratic community.

Alternative Education Curriculum

It is ...useful for educators to comprehend the changing conditions of identity formation within electronically mediated cultures and to appreciate how they are producing a new generation of youth which exists between the borders of a modernist world of certainty and order, informed by the culture of the West and its technology of print, and a post-modern world of hybridized identities, electronic technologies, local cultural practices, and pluralized public spaces. (Giroux, 1996, p. 61)

If the purpose of a traditional approach toward the education of our youth has been to continue the dominance of the current culture (Bourdieu, 1993; Posner, 1995), then the values that are represented by that curriculum's pedagogy are designed to conserve the fabric of the culture. This is to say that the traditional curricula perpetuate culture along the lines of cultural reproduction theory (Bourdieu, 1993). Those in power exercise influence to maintain dominance; therefore, conservative viewpoints perpetuate the economic and social conditions that brought the leaders of the culture to their current status and position. In the words of Cummins and Sayers (1995), "Curricular content and its mode of presentation represents one aspect of the way education is structured. In the not-so-distant past, much of the curriculum in North American schools was unashamedly Eurocentric and in many cases explicitly racist" (p. 381).

The conservative argument is also furthered by pervasive societal fears that not only is our economic well-being jeopardized by a faulty educational system, but the very democratic ideals that we have worked so long and hard to attain may be lost to an unruly, illiterate populace (Giroux and McLaren, 1989). The writings of E. D. Hirsch (Hirsch, Kett, and Trefil, 1991), and former Education Secretary William Bennett's terse report *A Nation At Risk* (National Commission on Excellence in Education, 1983) both exemplify the fears of the future changes within our cultural and educational realities. This alliance of conservative thinkers is eloquently articulated by Michael Apple (1995), who states:

This policy block combines business with the new Right, with neoconservative intellectuals, and with a particular fraction of the management oriented new middle class. Its interests are less in increasing the life chances of women, people of color, or labor. (These groups are obviously not mutually exclusive.) Rather, it aims to provide the educational conditions believed necessary both for increasing our international competitiveness, profit, and discipline and for returning us to a romanticized past of the "ideal" home, family, and school. (p. ix)

Joining Apple in opposing such conservative curricular and social reproductionist positions are an emerging group of educators who are calling for a new curriculum that speaks to the needs of our incipient culture (Apple, 1995; Giroux, 1996; McLaren, 1997; Wink, 1997). Called critical educators or pedagogists, this postmodern and radical group of educators have combined the thinking of Dewey, Bourdieu, and Freire in, "Rejecting the traditional view of instruction and learning as a neutral process antiseptically removed from the contexts of history, power, and ideology…" (Giroux and McLaren, 1989, p. xxi). From this perspective, the goals of critical pedagogy are to infuse meaning and culture into all aspects of the curriculum to develop relevance and purpose. These goals follow a larger philosophy or societal goal to successfully include all societal members, not just the elite.

Although it should be apparent that our nation's democratic ideals embody egalitarian principles, the general practice of educators within the United States has been to foster competition and to kowtow to the icons within our most elite institutions. Designing core college preparation to meet the needs of the University of California when only a scant four percent of California's high school students will gain admission is an example of perpetuating exclusion. The excellence strategy leaves ninety percent of the student body frustrated and alienated from feelings of future success. DeVillar (1994) captures the irony of our ideals gone awry:

The problem has been that we confuse the national ideal toward which we should always strive (the melting pot model) with actually having achieved this state, when we operate as a nation in accordance with the principles reflected in the Anglo-American conformity model. If this is indeed the case, then how does the Anglo-American identity model differ from the melting pot national identity image? Essentially, the Anglo-American conformity model is exclusive rather than inclusive, and group selection has been perennially and inexorably tied to color. (p. 45)

Against a backdrop of racism and unequal opportunities, some new voices in American education are seeking inventive ways to reach our disenfranchised and marginalized youth to help them break from cultural reproduction of school failure (Giroux, 1996; McLaren, 1986). To this end, the cultural studies curriculum includes elements that may contribute to cultural growth and a more democratic realization of our ideals. My view of cultural studies incorporates the perspective of Cummins and Sayers (1995) that "...educational reform can be effective only when it actively challenges the real causes of under achievement, which are rooted in the social conditions of schools and communities" (p. 9).

Cultural studies achieves the break with traditional, subject-centered curricular approaches by allowing the teacher and the student to critically examine the world around them through the lens of our diverse culture. In the challenging world of school change (Sarason, 1990), cultural studies provides a curricular framework filled with educational purpose (Dewey, 1916; Posner, 1995), epistemological principles (Posner, 1995), and the psychological strength to successfully reframe schools to become the truly democratic institutions that they can be. As the demographics of our schools change from a white majority to numerical dominance of minority groups, it is essential that we incorporate multicultural and critical pedagogy within our schools (see Figure 2).

The spokespersons for cultural studies concur in their goals yet differ in their approach. Cummins and Sayers (1995) advocate the use of technology such as the Internet as a furthering of the work of Freinet's modern school movement. Freinet believed in a process of learning that was reinforced through interaction with the environment and the establishment of meaning through reflected cultural study (Cummins and Sayers, 1995). Philosophically, Freinet stood with progressives such as Dewey and the existentialists who characterized the French intellectual community in the middle of the twentieth century.

Figure 2: K-12 Enrollments in Public Schools by Ethnicity

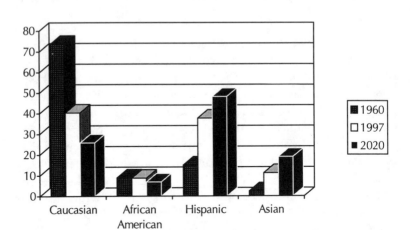

In the United States, Dewey's influence has inspired a reconstructionism that has led to the emergence of the postmodern school of educational reform. This movement to develop reforms to build new schools for the twenty-first century has focused on critical literacy and pedagogy to create curriculum for our diverse constituency. The role of cultural studies in this movement is paramount. Although the curriculum of cultural studies is sometimes vaguely defined, its importance lies in its attempt to refute the hidden curriculum (Giroux, 1983) and to openly relate our current social issues to the lives of our students in the most relevant manner.

As an example of how cultural studies can be integrated with the curriculum, I used Woody Allen's film *September* to connect the topic of depression to the curriculum of a graduate seminar in assessment in counseling. My motive was to show that depression could be assessed informally through observations of behavior and of the use of language. The film naturally lent itself to the observation process. Students were able to identify many elements of clinical depression in the protagonist. Further discussion concluded that the dearth of commercial film dedicated to the topic of depression may connect to a cultural pattern of the denial of depression's prevalence as the most frequently occurring form of mental illness within the American psychological landscape.

Although the influence of cultural studies in the context of traditional, subject-centered courses may seem at first to be tangential, I believe that the influence is profound. Bringing in the experience of art, drama, film, and other literary devices allows for the development of personal and culturally specific meaning (Bourdieu, 1993). This connection supports the postmodern, critical pedagogist's contentions of the essential need to develop multicultural collaborations in support of literacy (Taxel, 1989). Curriculum that is organized to feature involvement in the areas of social bonding and relevance (Posner, 1995) makes a subject more engaging.

Cultural studies works well as a counternarrative to official (hegemonic) or operational curriculum (Posner, 1995) by allowing the introduction of current and culturally relevant experience to the lessons. This interjection of creativity is essential in engaging at-risk learners. Whereas traditional curriculum may tend to control the direction of the transmission of knowledge (Cummins and Sayers, 1995) along a course of cultural reproduction (Bourdieu, 1993), cultural studies challenges the hidden curriculum's denial of our need to address the issues of "multiculturalism, race, identity, power, knowledge, ethics, and work" (Giroux, 1996, p. 44).

Cultural studies also challenges the null curriculum (Posner, 1995). The null curriculum includes those courses that are not taught because of their infringement on the traditional four content areas: language, math, science, and history. Cultural studies posits that, "...we have entered a period in which the traditional distinctions that separate and frame established academic disciplines cannot account for the great diversity of cultural and social phenomena that has come to characterize an increasingly hybridized, postindustrial world" (Giroux, 1996, p. 46).

Cultural studies offers a true bottom-up approach (Posner, 1995) to curriculum change. This experiential methodology is well suited for the unique needs of the at-risk youth that we serve in alternative schools. The hands of alternative school teachers are not as tied as are those of the teachers in secondary schools built around the structure of the disciplines (Posner, 1995). Cultural studies also deserves a place within the academy as a way to exhibit the values of multiculturalism and modernist thinking. Only through experientially displaying our ability to make the connections between knowledge and function can we, as a society, proceed in a different way. Cultural studies provides the vehicle to reconstruct not only our schools, but our other social institutions as well. Because culture is neither deterministic nor static (Nieto, 1996), the dynamic qualities of cultural studies provide a perfect fit for such a context.

The alternative school must prepare all students to achieve basic, minimum competencies while keeping them in school. To ensure learning, individualized instruction needs to be implemented. Individualization is keyed to successful instruction because many of the alternative education students are functioning on a grade level dissimilar from their grade placement. Some educators theorize that within any single classroom distribution there may be as much variability in grade placement as one year for each grade represented. That is, in a tenth grade classroom, there will be ten years of grade difference represented. The reading levels vary from grades two to twelve. In an alternative education setting, that estimate may be an understatement! To approach that group with anything other than an individualized plan could create chaos. Third grade readers, no matter how much you've prepared them with sensitivity to their needs, will destroy your lesson if you're expecting them to read on an eighth grade reading level.

The best way to determine the reading level of a text is to conduct your own assessment. This can be done by a simple calculation—counting the number of syllables within a passage and dividing by the number of words. Obviously, multisyllabic words are more difficult to read and require greater experience and decoding skill. A quick Cloze test will reveal the level at which your readers comprehend the texts you wish to use. To build a Cloze test, leave each seventh word (except definite or indefinite articles) out of a sample of text that you typically teach. If students can substitute an appropriate word, they demonstrate comprehension of the text. Although these techniques are often presented in a semester course on the teaching of reading, you may get some crash information from your school psychologist or special education staff. Individualizing the reading program is the only way I know to build reading success (Smith, 1978).

One of the lessons I have learned from teaching disaffected youth is that they are developmentally delayed as well as educationally deficient. The impact of years of substance abuse, truancy, and nonparticipation in learning keeps these students from achieving personal growth in all areas. They appear to be mature, but their social reasoning skills, decision-making skills, and self-esteem are often more characteristic of those of preadolescents. A student-centered curriculum works best to teach and reach these students. Using a team teaching approach, the alternative school can focus on the needs of the individual first and the content of the curriculum second. As with the early adolescent, the challenge of the alternative school is to change the self-esteem of its learners and to teach them with innovative and effective methods.

Many educators have found that the process of "integrated learning" has much to contribute to middle school–aged and alternative education students (Eggebrecht et al., 1996). According to Eggebrecht (1996), "...integration provides engaging experiences in which students encounter essential content in multiple and meaningful contexts in response to their own inquiry" (p. 5). Integrated learning uses the natural curiosity of students to motivate them to learn. As in Bruner's thematic teaching (Bruner, 1966), students can participate in the learning of seminal skills through the process of exploring projects that are both grand and motivating.

Experiential learning also reinforces relevancy and enriches the learning process (Rogers, 1969). Experiential process, although everything we do is an experience, implies active learning. Learning by doing helps kinesthetic learners as well as those who learn best through auditory and visual modalities. This type of learning has been popularized by Outward Bound and Project Adventure (Gass, 1993; Rohnke, 1981). Many alternative schools in the United States and abroad use techniques that are based upon this philosophy. This methodology is especially effective in the teaching of life skills (Moote and Wodnarski, 1997). Life skills, according to Brown and Mann (as cited in Moote and Wodarski, 1997) are those abilities that include the self-efficacy, communication skills, and problem-solving abilities that are critical to the successful functioning or adaptive behavior of the individual.

Relevance continues to be a fundamental issue in an alternative setting. Students benefit from reading about specific content areas and relating their reading to their topic of interest. For example, a student who is interested in whales can read about whales, write about whales, and research whales to achieve their desired knowledge. Additionally, all reading that is individualized and directed toward vocational or recreational interest has purpose and improves reading (Smith, 1978).

Math also needs to be taught using the most highly motivating methods. Just as with reading programs, the successful math program needs to be individualized. Coxford and Hirsch (1996) state, "The individual work accommodates differences in ability, interest, and mathematical knowledge, and challenges students in heterogeneous classes" (p. 25). The salient goal in all instruction is to motivate and inspire student interest.

Most high school students feel that they should study algebra, and there is no reason why an algebra course cannot be adapted to accommodate a greater number of students rather than acting to weed out those who are not "mathletes" (Alper, Fendel, Fraser, and Resek, 1996). But call the math what you will, teaching the same long division or fraction exercises will result in the same student outcomes: failure.

A lot of the fun for teachers is in developing specific courses to address the psychological and social needs of these students. Courses in life decisions, health science, psychology, communication, outdoor education, community service, understanding cultural diversity, our environment, and conflict resolution can provide the impetus to learn the reading, math, writing, and socialization skills these students must have to survive. To call the classes by the same old names is to reinforce the resistance that an alternative education student loves to express.

In the period before I moved to California, I taught outdoor education in the Wonalancet Alternative School (the Alt). The motto of the Alt School was, "Fuck that shit!" That motto was a true reflection of how my students felt about traditional education! Our challenge as educators was to devise curriculum that didn't evoke that expletive as a response. The student's challenge was to extinguish schoolwork that made them miserable and to reinforce us when we provided lessons that were enjoyable for them to complete. I appreciate the fact that often the learning was two-way. We both had opportunities to grow.

The Wonalancet Alternative School

> We all find comfort applying familiar solutions to problems, sticking to what we know best.... After all, if the solution were easy to see or obvious to everyone, it probably would have already been found. (Senge, 1990, p. 61)

I joined the staff of the Wonalancet Alternative School (the Alt) in the fall of 1985. The staff comprised a director, Kerry Goldstein; an academic teacher, Charles Fowler; an aide, Janet Hathaway; and an outdoor education teacher, me. Occasionally our staff was supported by a part-time teacher or a counselor during times of large enrollment. Large for us was fifty-five students.

The students chosen for the Alt were selected by counselors at the comprehensive high school, Wonalancet High School. Wonalancet was a school with an enrollment of approximately 1,000 students. Ninety-nine percent of the student body was Caucasian. The alternative education students were chosen from the cohort of students who had failed ninth grade. Many of these students were considered to be conduct disordered, and they were well known to the high school administrators. From that freshman cohort, we attempted to select twenty students whom we felt would be successful in our program. They would become our core group.

The core students would spend a year or more with us. They would take all of their academic classes with the alternative school staff. Outdoor education supplanted physical education. On Tuesdays and Thursdays the core would split in half. One half would go on an outdoor education field trip and the other half would stay at the Alt. Their schedule was a block type. Several periods were combined together so that our schedule was not dependent upon the bell. We could have the students for as much as eight hours at a time. In the case of our summer program, we had them for three weeks!

After successfully completing grade nine, our students could return to the alternative school to take a two-credit class called Life Decisions. This class was designed as a follow-up to the more intensive alternative core and as a way to maintain contact with our students. The class also included an outdoor education component. Because Life Decisions was a seminar-styled class, the students were free to discuss topics of interest to them. This requirement left the class loosely structured. It could be repeated in both the junior and senior years. One of the goals of the alternative school was to reconnect its students with the high school and to have them graduate from there. To this end, Life Decisions acted as a link between the Alt and the comprehensive high school.

The habitat selected for our alternative school was very successful in its ability to connect students with their teachers. The alternative school's building was an old colonial house. The house was vacant and located in back of the campus of Wonalancet High School, conveniently separated from the high school by a vocational building and a cemetery. For an alternative high school, the housing couldn't have been better. We had a kitchen in which to prepare meals and a homelike atmosphere. Most of all, we had large blocks of time to spend in the uniquely structured outdoor settings and within the alternative school itself. Those ingredients contributed greatly to the creation of a sense that the students were truly having an alternative school experience.

The staffing was an especially effective component of the alternative school. We almost always team-taught. Therefore, our staffing meant that two adults went on all trips and two adults stayed at school. This student-teacher ratio guaranteed that there was always a person free to talk with an individual student, to answer the phone, provide relief for a bathroom break, or to generally support the person who was teaching. Given the resistance that was often the companion to the alternative student's repertoire, the support of another adult was not a luxury, it was essential!

Our staff arrangement also recognized the importance of the influence of male and female staff persons working together. This balance was instrumental in developing feelings of familial support within the students. Often we were in the roles of nurse, counselor, listener, or surrogate parent. Because our success with the students was accomplished by acquiring their trust, having a gender balance and respectful relationships among ourselves had a significantly positive carryover with our students. Trust (Bates, Chung, and Chase, 1996) was enhanced because we had the time and the sensitivity to address the personal needs of our students. Conversely, when we were not exhibiting our most positive and professional behavior, the students used that opportunity to reinforce negative attributes concerning the teacher, the work, or the school as a whole. Fortunately, discord among our staff was rare.

One of our earliest discoveries as teachers was that schoolwork was best accomplished at the moment. Readings that spanned a period of twenty to forty minutes were more successful than lengthy articles or full books. The average attention span of our students coincided perfectly with that strategy. We also learned that homework was never completed. Homework is an example of the type of cultural capital that our students lacked. Home life for alternative education students often lacks the protective features they need to complete homework assignments: quiet, space, and support. Therefore, assignments that were due the next day were a sure flop. The best practice was to have an activity that lasted about twenty minutes and then to move on to another. If the activity was a winner, great! If it was not a winner, then no one had to suffer through it for long.

Assignments that were tied to themes were more successful than work that was done in isolation or did not seem to be related to any larger issue. When the student's "boredom button" was pushed, their internal alarms would rouse them to full resistance! However, if entertainment could somehow be tied to the assignment, it was a guaranteed winner. The best example of what grabbed our students' attention had to do with a local blues musician, T. J. Rawlins. T. J. would come to the alternative school on a regular basis. His lessons would fuse the topics of rock and the blues with stories about the old bluesmen of the south who worked their way across the country. The students were fascinated to learn how rockers from Elvis to Eric Clapton got their styles by emulating various obscure bluesmen. T. J. would mesmerize the students by playing his guitar and demonstrating styles that exemplified the connection between rock and the blues. The music experience led naturally to further discussion of history and related language arts activities.

The film *Crossroads* is a good example of a language arts activity that was a natural follow-up to T. J.'s work with the students. After T. J. would come to the Alt, we would show the film *Crossroads* to reinforce the stories that T. J. shared and give additional credence to the role that the bluesmen played in the evolution of rock history.

Whenever we could include a current film in the construction of a lesson or a unit, student interest was markedly increased.

The timely manner in which the work was introduced was also very closely related to the probability that it would get done or be met with a tsunami of resistance. We learned that if the students came to us with unresolved feelings from any earlier encounters or interactions, those feelings would continue to hover about until they were resolved. It mattered not how enthralling our lesson was. If two of our students were angry at one another, those issues needed to be addressed before any teaching could take place!

Therefore, to facilitate any business or learning that needed to be attended to, we would start our afternoon session with a whole-class meeting. The meeting would begin with a teacher or a student going to the blackboard and listing everyone's agenda for the day. Of course, the teachers would say, math, social studies, and the like. The students would interject break, movie, or whatever was on their minds. We'd then divide up our time and vote on what went where in the day. Then we'd all try to follow the schedule. This worked well to democratize the experience and empower the students in the process of their own education. This experience gave the students a voice and feelings of validity in the process of their learning!

One of my former students, Raylene Johnston, summed up the importance of being able to deal with her feelings and the benefit that process provided. Raylene said, "Like most of the kids that were there, I had a hard time coping with my feelings and the life that I had been living. (At the Alt) I was given the freedom to feel any way I needed to at the moment. I was also given the freedom to have space to deal with it. Rather than be carted off for inappropriate behavior, I was shown a better way. I felt like I had the freedom to ask for what I needed. I learned how to express myself in my own unique way, how to have respect for others." Raylene concluded, "When you learn (to) trust the small group around you, you will find something of your own trust and self-worth." These learnings demonstrate how the process of listening to our students developed into the substantive social learning that made our program effective.

In addition to our teaching counseling style, we found that the more relevant and engaging the topic of study, the more our students would get involved. When they had a successful day, it was very apparent in their faces. Conversely, when the students hated a lesson, we would have to teach through the gales of resistance. There is a lot of learning for a teacher in an alternative setting. Much creativity is required as well as a very thick skin.

When I started at the alternative school, I was filled with excitement and idealism. I had wanted that outdoor education job since the school first opened in the 1970s. After I was hired, I was on cloud nine! However, after I met the students, I was shocked at the amount of resistance I encountered. The students basically said that they weren't ready to accept me as their new outdoor education teacher. They liked the old one, and they didn't want to follow me or any of the rules that I had established for them. The students informed me that the old teacher didn't make them do such and such. The old teacher was cool, and the old teacher understood them. In a nutshell, I didn't know what I was doing.

After hitting such a wall of rejection, I ended up one afternoon in one of the school counselor's offices and bawled for an hour. I couldn't believe that I was fool enough to take that job at the alternative school! The students were rejecting me, and I felt like a failure! The counselor was a great comfort to me. She knew the students that I was teaching, and she said that their resistance was normal. My job was to accept them as they were and then they would accept me. I needed to stop trying to make them into something they weren't. The expectations that I had were unrealistic.

The adjustment that I made over the ensuing weeks and months improved my ability to win the students' trust and respect. I continued to learn about my students and to try to see the world through their eyes. Through understanding their point of view, I was able to meet the students in the middle between their ability to work and conform to rules and my ability to communicate a warmth and affection for them no matter what they felt about the given tasks. Why I thought the students would accept me unconditionally when I wouldn't do that for them stands out as one of the most naive notions of my career! The students and I both needed to come to the point of accepting each other through a natural process.

A good example of the way we both would be flexible had to do with their expressions. Almost without fail, on a trip to the beach, the mountains, a museum, whatever, a student would say, "This trip sucks!" The expression got to me. It seemed that no matter what we did, the same response would unveil itself. I had to take action. I called the students aside and I said, "Hey! I'm confused. When I hear 'sucks' I'm thinking something different than what you're saying. I think that if something 'sucks' then it's fantastic! So if you want to tell me that you don't like a trip, think of another way of saying it."

The students thought that my pronouncement was hilarious, and they went along with the joke. Slowly, they began to change their expression. If they liked the trip they would say, "This trip sucks!" That exclamation would be accompanied with a big smile. If they didn't like the trip they'd say, "It's awesome!" The reversing did much to mitigate my frustration with hearing the constant complaints. With oppositional students, we have to experiment with turning their resistance into something more tolerable for both the students and the teachers. Spinning the expression is much more productive for everyone rather than trying to deny them. Arguing with oppositional and defiant students is an invitation for defeat. These students are not going to be denied their expression, and that's one of their charms. We may not like what they are saying, but they are honest.

Alternative education students carry considerable frustration. They are angry to have failed in the traditional system, and they are unsure of their ability to succeed. The result is a confusion about where to place their blame; on themselves or on the system that did this to them. This phenomenon I call the "failed" student's dilemma. Letting go of the blame and anger is a hard process. To travel from anger and self-hate to acceptance and self-respect is the eternal quest. Since Plato's dictum to "know thyself," teachers of the humanities have struggled to find the way to help students learn how to develop a congruent identity and a positive sense of self. In alternative education, it is the continual and quintessential goal.

One of the best examples of a method to allow the venting of student anger came serendipitously on a gray March day. Lying innocently beneath us on the Alt school's basement floor was a large number of old metal folding chairs. Because they were school property and symbolically significant, the chairs took on one last use for our students.

Matt appeared in the Life Decisions class with a load of rage on that March day. After failing to mitigate his anger with the usual counseling strategies, we discovered the chair's last use. I suggested to Matt that he take one of the chairs from the basement, bring it out to the driveway in front of the school, and destroy it. This appealed to Matt. He took the chair outside and spent the better part of thirty minutes pounding the chair into the asphalt. Vented and sweaty, he came back into the class relieved. The process became known as "Doing a chair." The point of the process was that it gave recognition to the feeling of anger and it legitimized the process of venting one's anger against a tangible object and not hurting oneself in the process. So often, our students would be carrying anger only to have the release of that anger come back and hurt them further. A good example of that was when an angry boy would punch a wall or other hard object only to hurt himself more. Other examples of personal abuses abound; drug abuse, fights, body carving. Having an awareness of the true use of intervention strategies that work for alternative education students is the difference between being able to survive as an observer to the wars they are waging or falling victim to the student's own undermining of their progress and education. At the Alt School, we were constantly experimenting with our methodologies to find pragmatic and psychologically correct techniques to help our students find successful solutions to their real-life problems.

Setting the Emotional Tone

> The cerebrum works fully only as threat is absent. The settings for
> brain-compatible education must be as free from threat as possible, not
> simply by good intention but by inherent design. (Hart, 1983, p. 132)

The emotional tone of an alternative school is critical to the school's success. The development of feelings of support and trust between the students and the faculty is the single most significant component in the change process for the alternative education student (Prouty, Radcliff, and Schoel, 1988). Whereas these students once looked at education as an adversarial process because they only experienced the negative consequences of their inappropriate behavior, they now need to be convinced of the sincere desire of school staff to be allies in their success.

The most important element in reversing the student's sense of failure is to demonstrate the school's understanding of the "failed" student's dilemma. Adolescents are notorious either/or thinkers. Their experience is most often expressed as black or white. Therefore, teenagers will usually be giving either one of two opinions. The response tends toward "This is awesome!" or "This sucks!" Adults, too, can fall victim to the trap of reductionistic either/or thinking. In the case of a "failed" student, the reason for school failure is often placed squarely on the shoulders of the student. Educators have become proficient at placing the responsibility for student failure outside the school. Examples of blaming the victim abound. "The parents don't support the teachers or demand that the student complete homework." "The student doesn't attend frequently enough to earn credit to pass." "Despite modification, the student is not completing any of the work." These examples of reductive thinking resound in schools. Denial of the school's complicity protects the school from change.

The "failed" student's dilemma lies in overcoming the irony that they have been to blame for their school failure for the past eight or ten years. Why now would the new teachers treat them differently? Countering the blame of the schools, the student's response to the either/or summation has been to conclude that school sucks. In order to overcome the naturally ingrained resistance on the part of the alternative education student, special understanding is required. The students need to let go of their ingrained assumption that they will be to blame if their school experience does not change for the better and that the school is a damned place for its historic condemnation of them. These realities require special expertise in psychological understanding and, often, personal counseling finesse, to overcome the resistance that often accompanies these formerly failed students.

One of the solutions to reversing low self-esteem because of school failure is built upon demonstrated student successes. Success is first experienced through the development of a positive relationship with the teacher and then through a positive relationship with the work (Kohl, 1994). There is the belief within the student that he or she is safe (Hart, 1983) and that it is possible for them to achieve success.

Key to the development of trust at the Wonalancet Alternative School was the establishment of a few, simple rules. The first and foremost of the rules was: No put-downs. Put-downs include the entire range of racial, ethnic, gender, intellectual, and other comments meant to place one student above another in a verbal joust. Put-downs are the leading cause of fights, disruption, and chaos in most groups and families. Often, the put-down is an expression of anger that is thinly disguised as a joke. Called "doing the dozens" within the African American community, this experience is contrived to build a shield of defense against verbal abuse. In reality, the game is dangerous and leads to major social problems, not the least of which are fights.

Establishing the no put-down rule takes constant vigilance; however, the reward in terms of school climate is huge. We all can work to remind ourselves that none of us are any better nor any less than anyone else (Kopp, 1989). Our lives are experienced in communities defined by varying amounts of diversity. In this context, our individuality requires nurturing and acceptance. We are all human, capable of mistakes and, conversely, capable of experiencing the rewards of our correctness!

The second rule of the alternative school was that everything that was spoken about at the alternative school stayed at the alternative school (except as required by laws regarding child abuse). This rule reinforced the trust that we wanted to develop among the students. Often, on hikes or other trips, comments of a personal nature would slip out. We didn't want the students to feel that once a personal situation was revealed that the story would spread throughout the community. The confidentiality rule was hard to monitor, but the students generally respected it.

The significance of these two rules was in their emphasis on mutual respect and the protection of the individual. The value of these rules revealed itself in helping to establish a friendly tone in the Alt. Students certainly had their differences, but they were able to live in a culture based upon mutual respect.

Another component of the Alt that helped the tone was the genuine concern that the staff had for the students. All of the staff had the interest of the students first. Our philosophic position was that no teaching could occur until the students were ready to learn. This meant that we needed to be sensitive to their feelings at the beginning of each academic block. When we forgot the importance of that position and rushed ahead with our teaching agenda, the students reminded us of the preeminence of their feelings in the learning process by disrupting our lessons. There was no shortcut to the future with these students. The process of their education was equally as important as the end result—graduation.

A balance of gender, race, ethnicity, and other human qualities is essential to the tone of the school. An alternative school needs to reflect the positive values of the community that it serves and to be balanced accordingly. In this way the staff can model the benefits of diversity and help the students see the value everyone possesses. Balance contributes considerably to the development of a positive atmosphere within the school.

Although there are many factors that work together to shape the tone of an alternative school, the fact that a person's psychological feelings are preeminent cannot be overstated. Staff and students alike are the essential players in the development of the school's tone, spirit, and atmosphere. Without staff and administration efforts to enhance the resiliency qualities essential to adolescent growth and development, learning is an uphill battle, and the development of trusting relationships will never occur. The net result will be both student and school failure. Just how those resiliency factors are enhanced is the focus of the remainder of this text.

Alternative Education Methods

> Whether or not we are aware of it, there is nothing of which we are more ashamed than not being ourselves, and there is nothing that gives us greater pride and happiness than to think, to feel, and to say what is ours. (Fromm, 1941, p. 288)

Alternative education views the process of personal change and growth as dynamic. Although this process encompasses the mistakes and learnings of the past and aspires toward goals and benefits of a healthy future, alternative education exists in the here and now (Gaines, 1979). The focus is immediate and very much in the present tense. The actions of the moment and the challenges they present provide numerous opportunities to learn and grow. Successful alternative schools incorporate modern psychological and resiliency theories to create an atmosphere that fosters the trust that allows positive development to occur. According to Bonnie Benard (1991), "Just as in the family area, the level of caring and support within the school is a powerful predictor of positive outcome for youth" (p. 10).

Most students in an alternative setting are continually wrestling with issues that placed them in an at-risk position. The healing and recovery from abuse and self-defeating behavior requires a strong and supportive atmosphere that acknowledges the challenges of personal growth and the joy that can come from success. All students require safety and trust to learn (Maslow, 1968). For the at-risk student of today, these fundamentals must continually be acknowledged and reinforced (Hart, 1983).

To achieve success, alternative schools require wellness activities and a model that includes active student assistance. Support groups based on all of the major stresses (alcohol and other drugs, divorce, loss and separation, and low self-esteem) are vital tools to reinforce the notion that the school is committed to the student's recovery. The presence of support groups underlines the school's recognition of the preeminence of the feelings of these students in the process of reclaiming them for the learning of reading and math. To meet their needs for support and to develop resiliency within the students, the

Student Assistance Program (SAP) offers one of the most well-structured models of intervention. Articulated by Cheryl Watkins (Watkins, 1992), SAP is organized around six- to eight-week group encounters. The groups are structured to be able to be run by teachers who are trained in their implementation. In my experience, these groups are best facilitated by counselors. Because issues of great portent are often revealed in the groups, a counselor is best suited to understand the sensitive nature of each counselee's situation. Counselors are also trained to follow-up with further work as needed.

As a method, alternative education includes an evaluation of the student's needs (educational, vocational, psychosocial) and the establishment of a plan to successfully address those needs. This is a process of individualizing instruction and planning goals for graduation and learning beyond high school. This process also includes the student's family and an assessment of the family's needs (Soriano, Hong, and Mercado, 1996). When the family is included in planning and goal-setting, the student is supported by all of the significant players in their quest for success, and protective resiliency features are enhanced.

This inclusion of the family in the planning process needs to be systematized and formalized (Pianta and Walsh, 1996). All parents need to meet regularly with their child's teachers to discuss their progress and the means that need to be used to achieve student success (Pianta and Walsh, 1996). "A major risk factor that contributes to learning problems encountered by students, particularly in inner city schools serving students from diverse ethnic and cultural backgrounds, is the disconnection between schooling and family life" (Wang, Haertel, and Walberg, 1994, p. 60). The need to connect family and school to enlist the students for success is strongly supported in the literature (Comer, 1980).

To develop trust with the families, one must understand their culture and unique needs. Multicultural education must be a major component of the school's process. Hiring and all aspects of the school must be reflective of the constituency that the school serves. Parents are more likely to trust that members of the school staff truly want to involve them in the education of their child when they see their own family and cultural values reflected at the school (Nieto, 1996). Just as racism is not allowed by individuals within the school, the school also does not practice covert or institutional racism by not actively honoring the diversity within its community (Page, 1996).

Some of the finest contributions to the area of parent involvement have been posited by Norris Haynes and James Comer (Haynes and Comer, 1996). During the last twenty-five years, James Comer and a cadre of committed fellow educators have been researching the effectiveness of parent involvement. From a model called the School Development Program (SDP), Haynes and Comer call for three basic conditions that appear to be necessary for successful parent involvement. They state:

> Several conditions must exist for parental involvement to be successful. These are:
>
> 1. *Trust*: Basic to any attempt to reach and involve parents, especially the least affluent and educated, is the development of a climate of trust and openness to ideas. Parents sometimes avoid schools because they feel inadequate, unwelcome, threatened, or insecure due to their own past educational experiences and their children's present difficulties. In SDP (School Development Program) communities, we seize every opportunity to break down the barriers of distrust by reaching out to parents in their communities through home visits (with appropriate safeguards in high-risk neighborhoods); regular and positive telephone calls and memos; and networking through community institutions (such as churches, synagogues, or mosques), community groups, and support services agencies.
>
> 2. *Preplanning*: For parent involvement to be effective and successful, it must be carefully planned and coordinated to avoid confusion, anxiety, and disaster. School staff, through adequate representation on the SPMT (School Planning and Management Team) and direct input where feasible and necessary (as in the case where a parent is being paired with a teacher or assigned to work with a given staff member), must participate collaboratively with the administration when making decisions about the roles parents fill in the school. This process of collaborative planning helps to reduce or obviate tension and creates a climate of mutual respect and support.
>
> 3. *Empowerment*: In SDP communities, we provide opportunities for parents to participate fully in the life of the school, including planning and making decisions about the school's academic and social agenda, through their role on the SPMT and their contributions to the development of the comprehensive school plan. We give the parents a voice in helping to decide how to shape the minds and hearts of their children. We also give them the

opportunity to continually grow and develop and to reform their
habits of mind, heart, and work. (pp. 503–504)

Parent involvement with alternative education students,
however, is not a panacea. Many of the students' parents are more
dysfunctional than their children! Enlisting parent support for the
growth and change of the alternative education student needs to be
done in a carefully structured way. A lack of understanding of the
anger and volatility of a part of your parent constituency could lead
to potential public relations issues. Conversely, a strong and
supportive parent group can work well to enhance the program's
credibility with the school board and superintendent.

My favorite example of parent support working favorably has to
do with a school board request for an alternative summer school (see
Chapter 13). Because many of our students were repeating ninth
grade for the second or third time, we needed to develop a strategy
to accelerate their progress. Seeking support for a new program to
help our students graduate, a group of parents, students, and I came
before the board. This summer school program was very innovative
and required a considerable financial commitment from the school
board. I am convinced that the eloquent words of a few of our
parents were the compelling reason that the board approved the
program.

Alternative education philosophy and method provides each
student with opportunities to grow from self-defeat to self-
fulfillment. The word "alternative" implies that this process will be
uniquely and deeply personal and developed individually (Bomotti,
1996). For the entire community, we need all of our individuals to be
successful and productive members. Alternative education recognizes and celebrates cultural pluralism and the need for all to be
included in meaningful ways. This means equal opportunity for each
student regardless of ethnicity (Page, 1996), gender, and ability.
Apple (1995) underlines the necessity to include a truly democratic
process in the alternative school by suggesting:

If the development of clear alternative programs is essential, these
alternatives need to be based on the democratic strength that actually
exists in the United States. Without clear programs that seem to
provide for at least partial solutions to local and national problems,
"most people will accept the dominant view, which is inherently

undemocratic and anti-egalitarian." Thus, these programs need to be sensible not only to hard-core activists but to working people with families and jobs. (pp. 158–159)

The Methodology of Surprise

> Of the many remarkable and unique aspects of persons or selves, perhaps the most extraordinary lies in the apparent fact that a self is fundamentally tied up with his or her *attitude* toward life or life-value. (Brockelman, 1985, p. 16)

How shall we approach the oppositional and defiant? By surprise, and in a way that they have not been asked to learn before. When I began working at the alternative school, the principal of the high school, James Hawthorne, called me into his office and asked me how it was going at the alternative school. I told him that the students were a real challenge and that I had to think fast to come up with new techniques to get their attention. James asked for an example, and I hesitatingly offered this one. I told James that the students used the word "fuck" all the time and that I needed to develop a "fuck" lecture. James asked, "What's a fuck lecture?" I replied that in response to the gross overuse of the word I called my students together and said, "Hey, listen up! 'Fuck' is my favorite word, but you guys are going to ruin it for me. Everyday I hear, 'Oh, fuck. I've got to get my fuckin' lunch out of my fuckin' locker to go on a fuckin' trip in the fuckin' van....'" I said, "Whoa, you are going to ruin this word for me. If you want to say the word 'fuck' that is perfectly OK. But save it for something really good, like if a canoe fell on your foot or something!" The student response was to stare at me with their mouths agape. Then came the comment, "That's cool."

James thought that this story was one of the funniest things he'd ever heard in his tenure as principal. For months after our meeting, I would be somewhere and be approached by someone who recalled my "fuck" lecture. Showing that you can waltz to the edge of the envelope on occasion builds your credibility with the alternative education student. However, for your own professional security, you may want to check out some of the local linguistic norms first.

Swearing or obscenity is defined, psychologically, as displaced aggression. Displaced aggression is a term from Freudian psychology that defines the concept of displacement (Hunt, 1993). If, for example, a student were angry at themselves for their current straits, that anger could more easily be released by swearing at some object or external person. Because alternative education students almost always carry anger as a form of personal baggage, the attendant strings of obscenity are a natural vent.

The other aspect of obscenity that bears regard relates to the local norm. I come from a part of New England where the weather could foul the tongue of a saint, where the "F'" word is often used merely as punctuation. Exclamation becomes, "Oh, fuck!" Interrogatives degrade to, "What the Fuck?" My biggest culture shock came after moving to the Central Valley of California, an area where white, middle-class values predominate. Here the use of the "F" word is reserved for gutters and prisons. I made the mistake of using the word during an Individual Educational Plan meeting with some of my new colleagues. The resultant meeting with my supervisor was most instructive! I confess to still being linguistically challenged at times when there just doesn't seem to be a better word, but in deference to my survival needs, I try to be careful and pick my spots for that pleasant indiscretion.

Because language and image are so intertwined, at the Alt School I tried to strike deals with my students to keep the language appropriate to the situation. In the woods, and far removed from civilization, the linguistic standards were different than they were in the classroom or in the local grocery. The rationale was respect; respect for ourselves and the alternative school as a whole. The students' learning where to chance an obscene gesture or phrase became a part of the larger game: being a teenager.

True to the nature of adolescence, risk is one of the teenager's favorite companions. In the domain of risk-taking, alternative education students pride themselves! Alternative education students are very desirous of adventure and challenge; they are fundamentals in a methodology first proposed by Kurt Hahn, refined by Willie Unsoeld, and used by Outward Bound. This methodology of outdoor and experiential learning well suits these heretofore resistant learners. Rock climbing, canoeing, skiing, and other outdoor activities give students the opportunity to satisfy their need to take risks. The outdoor education component was an essential part of what made our school alternative.

The outdoor-experiential approach also connects the students in a holistic way to their learning (Gass, 1993). Because it is lablike in structure, students are learning by doing (Luegers, 1997). The focus is upon the process of the learning, and participation and cooperation are the only requirements. In the language of adventure-based counseling, this is referred to as a part of the "full value contract" (Prouty, Radcliff, and Schoel, 1988). No one is devalued in the learning process.

One of the unique characteristics of the outdoor education approach is the way in which it can feature multiple invitations to rejoin a learning experience. Using a variety of positive methodologies, we break new ground away from memories of past failures. Within a supportive small-group atmosphere, the alternative school teacher can foster a relationship that can achieve positive results. Between 1970 and 1989, I spent approximately 150 days teaching climbing and rappelling at a local ledge called Stone House. One of New Hampshire's most beautiful sites, Stone House afforded excellent climbing; solid rock, gorgeous views, and infallible belays. Over the years, I developed a lesson and routine at Stone House that had a 100 percent success rate for getting students to rappel (Reif, 1984). I accomplished this success by telling all of the students that for some of them, rappelling wasn't scary at all. For the unafraid, because they trusted me, the exercise was just another thrill like riding a roller coaster. However, for a few of the students, showing up at the top of that two-hundred-foot cliff was the most courageous thing that they had ever done. We redefined success; everyone was a hero and the term "chicken" was never used. This methodology maximized the use of social psychological theory by including everyone in the process of the day. "Doing" became the best way to overcome a low sense of self-esteem that might make a student reluctant to participate. No one was devalued in the exercise.

Another successful tool to turn a "dropout" into a student is to let them be the teacher. The peer instruction method has been proven to be very effective for both teacher and learners. Among peer-centered adolescents, the focus shifts from the adult to their own (ownership) participation in the learning process. One of the keys to success in this methodology is that we are not perceived as interfering with their learning. With all students, we are most successful when we remember to be the "guide on the side," not the "sage on the stage."

The strategy that I have found to be the most effective for the teacher's personal and professional survival in dealing with at-risk youth is humor. The alternative education students have a great need to laugh and release frustration. The teachers, also, need to psychologically detach themselves from the immediate stress of their jobs to maintain their roles as good-humored participants. To serve these purposes, the constructive use of irony, paradox, and humor in a variety of forms (remember, no put-downs!) can make the difference between a disaster and success. Humor can provide the release necessary to keep an absurdity in its place. Often the alternative education student is facing multiple paradoxes and, of these, the "stupid" teacher is one they constantly watch for. Because they have been put-down many times by teachers, it is no wonder that students have developed the inverse of this hostility. By overstating our stupidity and showing our foibles, we allow the kids the opportunity to laugh at us in ways that enhance our relationship.

An example of the constructive use of humor relates to an old camp song. Often when we were in the woods, we would come across a beaver dam or lodge. To mark this event, I'd call the students together, point out the lodge, and sing, "The Beaver Song." The words are, "I'm a beaver, you're a beaver, we are beavers all; and when we get together we give the beaver call." For the finale of the song, you put your two index fingers in front of your mouth to simulate beaver's teeth and yell, "Hey!" This rendition's obvious silliness would always generate a flood of moans and laughs. Of course, the double entendre when I sang, "I'm a beaver" was not lost on many of our libidinous learners! The song became a part of the legend at the Alt.

Though it is not a methodology, per se, an understanding of the power and effect of alcohol can enhance understanding of one of the other dilemmas that alternative education students face. An alternative education parent may verbalize that they want their child to be successful in the world; however, the parent's alcoholism is a glaring example of their inability to overcome their own obstacles and have a healthy resolution of their problems. This irony can be interpreted in many ways, but students often misunderstand their parents' disease as a justifiable alienation from the world. The alcoholic parent blames the world for their own shortcomings. The boss fired them. The coach cut their son from the basketball team. In other words, the result of their effort or their child's effort is undermined by someone else. Blame is the defense of choice.

In any alternative school, more than several of the students will be coming from alcoholic and dysfunctional families. The rule in these families is chaos first! Don't count on anything! Dad could be home, or not. Mom could cook dinner, or be back in the hospital. This is a very insecure world. Because of their insecurity, any deviance from our school schedule hits these students right between the eyes. The message to them is: You are just like my parents; you are not trustworthy.

This "alcoholic" thinking of the parent is visited upon the child. "The world is wrong!" This child comes to school looking for the teacher to be the "deceiver." "What time do we do math?" "What time do we get to go to the bathroom?" Endless questions. I used to think that these students were put in my classes just to delay the class from starting! It took me years to see that these children of alcoholics were so insecure that they needed to know what was going to happen minute to minute, because in their personal lives, chaos was the clock. Life for them was totally unpredictable.

To be able to reach these students, tremendous understanding and patience is required. Again, humor can be the fuel that keeps the engine of education going when the resistance is running at its highest. My favorite example of how the changing of the schedule can cause a predictable fury and how humor can be used to diffuse it has to do with one afternoon at the alternative school. The basic schedule for the alternative school was generally predictable, although students and staff would negotiate the order of the day's activities. Monday was an academic day. Tuesdays and Thursdays were trip days. Wednesday was a movie day, and Friday was, well, TGIF!

One Wednesday, the academic teacher, Charles, usurped control of the daily calendar and declared that there would not be a movie that afternoon because he was behind in his teaching chronology. He dictated that there would be a math test in place of the movie. The students went wild. They declared, "You can't take away our movie!" "You're not fair!" The upshot of all of this is that they stormed out of the classroom and mulled around outside the building, smoking cigarettes and complaining. In a word, they went on strike. One girl even made a picket sign that said, "No Movie...No Test...Fuck Math!"

After giving the students time to vent, my response was to get a camera and to go out and join the strikers. One of my favorite momentos from the alternative school is a picture of myself making the worst face I can make and holding the sign of protest. Shortly after I joined the strike it dissolved. It dissolved because adults got involved. The protest wasn't against anything anymore. For an oppositional and defiant teenager, nothing wrecks a party more than adult permission and consent.

This example of the strike illustrates the two issues of schedule and oppositional behavior. Alternative education students are with us because they are not compliant. Realizing that, we need to not fuel their defiant nature by changing their schedule. A school works when it enlists the participation of its students. In an alternative setting, this requires finesse. Throwing a change in the schedule does no more than create angst.

When they understand the student's dilemma, alternative school educators can use humor to diffuse real and imagined catastrophes. Having the ability to see things differently has to be a key characteristic of an alternative school educator. This ability to work with conduct disorder is one of the premier skills of a successful alternative education teacher. As the students at the Wonalancet Alternative would proudly disclaim, "What the fuck! I go to the Alternative School!" We, the staff, would sometimes echo, "What the fuck? We teach there!"

CHAPTER 9

The Environment for an Alternative School

>...alternative schools pose some fundamental challenges to the way
>we organize and coordinate education. They call for diversity in
>preference to common standards and conformity. (Raywid, 1995, p. 31)

The ideal environment for alternative education invites discovery
and doing. It inspires curiosity and participation because students
are actively engaged in their education. Because of the unique needs
of alternative education students, they require an environment that is
not reminiscent of the one where they previously experienced failure.
In my experience, atmospheres that are close to nature, or natural
environments, provide the greatest opportunity to establish a
mindset conducive to learning. The value of differing environments
is strongly supported in educational research literature (Kellmayer,
1995; Young, 1990). The modern educational system has created
many examples of learning environments that diverge from the
traditional classroom, such as science labs, shop classes, demonstration kitchens, gymnasiums, outdoor learning centers, and technology
labs. As noted by Cairns and Cairns (1994), "The lessons are not
restricted to the classroom..." (p. 259).

Because we want to develop a more responsible and positively
engaged citizen, we need to help these students see applications of
their learnings outside the classroom and in relationship to a real-
world setting. The best subjects include those relevant to the lives of
the students and their families. The biggest gripe of at-risk students
is that the schoolwork and teachers in a traditional setting are not
related to their lives. In MacLeod's ethnography, *Ain't No Makin' It*,
the quotes of some of the "Hallway Hangers" sum up this sense of
alienation well.

>Chris: I hate the fucking teachers. I don't like someone always telling
>me what to do. Especially the way they do it. They make you feel like
>shit. I couldn't take their shit. (MacLeod, 1995, p. 108)

Whatever the setting, be it outdoor or in a career lab, the ideal
environment for at-risk students is one that reflects their dynamic

and physical nature. The appearance of the traditional classroom reinforces reminders of their experience of the past. Many of these students have Attention Deficit Disorder, anxiety disorders, learning disabilities, and/or impairments in their mental process. Placing them in an environment that produces déjà vu does not convince them that this is any "alternative." It looks like the same old structure in a different location or, as is the case in some districts, the location isn't even all that different. The alternative education classroom is often on the same campus as the mainstream school.

The first place alternative education should look for constructive change is in its environment. John Kellmayer's (1995) recent work on alternative schools places great emphasis on the value of setting for students. Kellmayer states, "The richer the site, the more powerful the effect of the site on modifying the cognitive and affective performance of at risk students" (p. 93).

Of all possibilities, the outdoors offers one of the best choices for alternative education. John Muir invites, "Climb the mountains and get their good tidings. Nature's peace will flow into you as sunshine flows into trees" (Teale, 1954, p. 311). My first work in an alternative high school was as an outdoor education teacher at the Wonalancet High School in Port Dover, New Hampshire. For three to five days a week, I'd load up to ten students and another adult into a twelve-passenger van, and away we'd go. We were located on the campus of the comprehensive high school; administrators would often breathe a sigh of relief to see the students that I had with me leaving the campus for the day!

We would leave the confines of the high school campus and cruise off to mountains, seasides, rock faces, and rivers for a day of adventures and misadventures. Overall, the students loved these trips. The trips provided a challenge and a release from the ordinary. These adolescents loved risk-taking, and the outdoor education program provided plenty of opportunity for adventure. Whether the student's challenge was climbing up the icy mountain or screwing up the hike's process, there was something they could sink their soul into and get a response.

Above all, through the course of our experiences, we learned to respect and understand each other. There was not a single physical fight during my four years at the alternative school. We had disagreements, arguments, and even a walkout strike, but no fights. I feel that the role that outdoor education played in providing an outlet for some of the frustration was a key ingredient in the process of keeping everyone going.

Not all alternative schools are as fortunate as those New Hampshire students in their proximity to natural habitats. However, the experience of getting out of the confines of a classroom is key to expanding the experience of the students. As Freinet used "learning walks" to inspire curiosity and develop literacy, the alternative school can incorporate outside experiences to build links with the community and enhance the inquisitiveness of its students.

Socialization is one of the major challenges facing an alternative education student. Oftentimes my students had not been exposed to experiences that I considered to be common. For example, a trip to a museum was met with resistance because of the preconceived notions of the students that they wouldn't fit there. Excursions to the city were also foreign. Restaurants other than McDonald's were odd. The entrenched attitudes that my students held were directly related to the dearth of experience they'd had. Fear of the unknown and unfamiliar were powerful forces that fed their racism, provincialism, and ignorance of the larger world around them.

In urban communities where fear is rampant, students and their families are even more alienated and fearful about the world around them. In his insightful ethnography of growing up as an African American in Portsmouth, Virginia, Nathan McCall (1994) wrote:

> Shortly after we moved in a neighbor warned my parents, "Be careful not to drive through Academy Park. Them is some mean crackers over there. They'll stone your car and shoot at you for driving through there."
> One night, when I was about ten years old, a little girl my age was shot to death while sitting near a picture window in her living room on Freedom Avenue. The killing brought home the fact that, nice neighborhood or not, we still weren't safe in Cavalier Manor. (pp. 9–10)

In communities where safety is a concern, looking for protective factors and working to maintain them is an important role for the alternative school teacher. Without a sense of safety and trust within the immediate environment, higher functions such as learning will not be accomplished. To this end, the entire community is key to the enhancement and betterment of itself. Within the contexts of our multifarious environments, we must seek affirmations of the future of our students as well as our own. We cannot minimize the value of the environment in the overall development of alternative education strategy.

Alternative Education Service to the Community

> The trashed-out areas of our cities, the billboards on our highways that prevent us from seeing nature's beauty, the thoughtless destruction of buildings that have memory and a long past, and the construction of cheap housing and commercial buildings—these and countless other soulless ways of dealing with things indicate anger, a rage against the world itself. When our citizens spray paint a trolley or subway or a bridge or a sidewalk, clearly they are not just angry at society. They are raging at things. If we are going to understand our relationship with the things of the world, we have to find some insight into this anger, because at a certain level those people who are desecrating our public places are doing a job for us. We are implicated in their acting out. (Moore, 1992, p. 274)

If we are to be successful in our mission to prepare young adults for an opportunity to participate positively within the community, we need to help them develop a sense of values that reinforce their positive behavior. Bluesman, Taj Mahal (1969) says simply, "You don't miss your water until your well runs dry." For many of our young, freedom is not appreciated until they have experienced incarceration. Many students in alternative schools have already experienced the loss of innocence, freedom from chemical dependency, and the ability to learn; they run hard to escape their reality only to find themselves in similar or worse situations.

To reunite these students with a positive sense of values and personal character, the use of community conservation activities provides powerful metaphors for saving the people as well as the planet. Making something better and seeing improvement demonstrates that those two possibilities do in fact exist. This is not a trite observation for alternative education students. For them, it is just short of a miracle.

Many opportunities exist for conservation activities that are lasting and meaningful. Building nature trails, improving wildlife habitats, and removing eyesores reinforce appreciation of the values of work. The pride of knowing, "I built that trail," reinforces further appreciation of future environmental and community interactions.

Many of the contributions of conservation advocates from our past (Theodore Roosevelt, Walt Whitman, John Muir, etc.) can be used to fill a much-needed void in our world today. Our youth need to know that there is a real world of beauty in nature that can accept and sustain them. What an opportunity for us to be able to lead students to explore and discover the secrets of nature.

Service to the community can take many forms. Helping at the local nursing home, peer tutoring in the elementary school, or removing graffiti from the school fence all reinforce the contribution that these students can make toward improving their lives and the environment that sustains them. Proven worth is essential to the healthy development of an alternative school student.

Often the alternative school student is quick to point out the absurdity and hopelessness in any situation. At first they do not understand why they should give anything to a community from which they feel alienated. How they could contribute to the community that has expressed little or no use for them does not make any sense to them either. In many ways this cognitive mindset matches the mental image of a depressive personality. The mindset is characterized by a pervasive sense of incongruence, and asks, "Where do I fit?" However, when they are faced with a person that values their company or skills, the alternative school student can stand just as proud as any other student.

As an example of how we worked to help our students to be more empowered, the staff at the Alt taught all of the students cardiopulmonary resuscitation (CPR). Just the same as any other activity, the lesson was met with a maelstrom of resistance. Initially, the students balked at the idea of "kissing" the dolls and said, "Why do we have to learn this" or "I'd never do that!" But eventually, even the most resistant complied. Almost all of our students successfully completed the course and were awarded their certificates.

On a spring day shortly after completing his CPR class, one of our alternative school students, Johnny, was visiting his grandparents at their home. Johnny told us, so as not to lose his status as an Alt student, that he was visiting them so he could borrow some money. During the visit, his grandfather had a heart attack in the backyard. Johnny was able to keep his grandfather alive by using the CPR he learned at the alternative school. It was a great day for everyone. When our students are heroes, it is a day for rejoicing!

Alternative education students need opportunities to prove their worthiness as citizens and as individuals. However, we, as teachers, need to remember that the connection between our students and this valuing process is often nonexistent. Because these students often lack the cultural capital to be accepted on their own, they need extra vigilance on our part to monitor their success. For example, they are preconditioned to be in a conflictual relationship with someone "from the other side." As they present themselves to the world, their posture is oppositional. For us to be successful in our work with alternative education students, not only do we need to be aware of their dilemmas, we also must recognize the need to structure the activities so the students can have the greatest possible chance for success.

The best method for discovering who will be receptive to the alternative education students is to go out into the community and experience interaction. Through the interactions with others within the community, teachers can find individuals or groups that can put alternative education students to work or play that is meaningful for both groups. When we left the Alt to go out on the road, we would often have little or no idea what we would find. After a while, we all came to call these trips, "the road to nowhere" after a song of the same name by the Talking Heads. On the road to nowhere, serendipity was the teacher's aide, and the community was the setting. During these trips, we would stop to explore areas that most of the world would drive by while traveling to and from work or personal business. Museums, nature preserves, lighthouses, parks, and old forts became our classroom.

Through these trips, the community took on a different meaning. It became a place to play and interact freely, and the possibility for a more personal and meaningful connection was created. Structured and protected by the staff, activity could occur that didn't end up in the familiar, negative ways.

The cult film *The River's Edge* was a film that we would regularly show at the Alt. Our students loved the film because they could relate to the themes of drugs, alienation, and angst that the characters portrayed. It is interesting to view *The River's Edge* with thoughts directed toward the relationship of the film's teenagers with their community. The adult with whom the teenagers had the most contact and who accepted them freely was the maniacal character Feck, played by Dennis Hopper. Feck lived alone and carried with him an inflatable woman. He was an insane paranoid whose mission was to supply the youth of the community with marijuana. Too often, in real life, our alternative education students ended up finding the Feck of their community. Fecks reinforce all of the alienation the students feel, and, as adults, they give the position a degree of credibility.

Against the backdrop of scenes such as those portrayed in *The River's Edge*, it is important that teachers use the opportunities that they have to be the best role models possible. According to Bonnie Benard (1991), "While the importance of the teacher as caregiver cannot be overemphasized, a factor often overlooked that has definitely emerged as a protective factor is the role of caring peers and friends in the school and community environments" (p. 10). Therefore, it is important that we seek out other, appropriate models within the community for our students to emulate.

When I taught at the Alt, I took the opportunity to use other voices as a way of reinforcing messages that I felt were important. In the area of drug and alcohol education, the area of utmost importance in the education of our students, a man named Johnny Long would visit and tell his story. When Johnny performed his "drunk-a-log," the students' ears would perk up. Many of our students could relate to the pain and loss that filled Johnny's life. Johnny, in his years of telling his story, grew skillful in identifying those students who could identify with his tales of alcohol's destruction of his career, self-respect, and family. Many students in both traditional and alternative education settings can relate to the tales that result from alcoholic lifestyles.

This connection with Johnny Long is an example of the power of using community resources. Whether the connection is through Alcoholics Anonymous, the community center, the local probation department, or any other agency in the community, links to successful experiences for alternative education students need to be discovered. It is only when our students experience success in the community that we will observe any significant changes in their attitude toward it.

The Human Element—Staffing

> My teaching would have been more effective if I had been able to engage in a critical analysis of those aspects of everyday life that resonated with and affirmed the dreams, desires, and histories of the students. (McLaren, 1994, p. 231)

As goes the adage about stepchildren always getting second best, so has been the experience of the alternative school. Often alternative schools have been staffed with teachers who have been ostracized from the comprehensive high school, and, like the students they teach, remanded to the alternative high school. It takes an enlightened administration to see that, ironically, not our worst teachers, but our best teachers need to earn their livelihood demonstrating their masterful skills in reaching and teaching the disaffected.

Teaching is a challenging and demanding profession, and it is at its most challenging and demanding level in the alternative school. Because of the special circumstances alternative education students present, alternative education teachers need to be acutely aware of how one can address the needs of this diverse and contentious learning community. Every day the possibility of your greatest "teachable moment" can flash before your eyes!

The chemistry of our staff at the Wonalancet Alternative School was especially well suited to the students we served. Our abilities to communicate with each other and to blend the often conflicting components of process and productivity led to a good balance of the two elements. Overriding all of the need for academic output was our commitment to student centeredness that is so critical to success. Legitimate concern for the well-being of our students transcended the requirements of a curricular framework. Our style was often more that of a counselor and coach than the tone of a traditional teacher. In fact, a traditional teaching voice elicited such a negative response that it was conditioned out of us by our energetic and enthusiastic teachers—those kids!

When you choose a staff for an alternative school, remember that counselors can contribute considerable expertise in the classroom.

Counselors can effectively use the psychological skills so necessary on an alternative school campus. By modeling an example of caring and of interpersonal communication skills, counselors can effectively reach students in a psychologically distinct manner. For example, counselors can often model the teaching of the psychosocial classes, such as health, conflict resolution, child development, and careers.

At the Alt, we found that classes that were team-taught modeled cooperative interaction. Skills for working together are critical in our culture. Alternative education students need to see that teamwork is the experience of working together and achieving a result greater than could be reached alone. This concept, synergy, as do all concepts with alternative education students, needs demonstration and constant reinforcement!

Although we frequently met frustration, our staff most often gained strength through cooperative teaching. The greatest benefit to me was the psychological lift that a colleague would give after a difficult class. Often another adult would have the distance and perspective on the students that I did not have because of my leadership position. For example, if some students were upset and I tried to teach through those feelings, I could end up perturbed as well. As Peter Senge (1990) states, "Structures of which we are unaware keep us prisoner" (p. 160). The other adult often was aware of the undercurrents of trouble, and, therefore, we could redirect each other. The process was continual.

The English primary method offers an addition appropriate to the alternative school. In the English primary model, the principal is the master teacher in the school. At the Alt, we enlisted this model. The school director was the master teacher. This model recognizes the unique needs for the continuing development of the alternative school staff and the strong, supportive leadership they require. Everyone, that is, the nurse, the counselor, and the administrator, needs to be in the classroom with these students. The point is that all of the staff and administration are in direct contact with students in positively structured ways every day. Students see the director in other contexts than a disciplinary one; the director models teaching in the toughest conditions. Alternative schools are quintessential learning organizations (Senge, 1990).

Working in an alternative school setting can often be fun because it provides a teacher with opportunities to apply innovative techniques. Almost everyone has given up on these students except you. You are, in all likelihood, one of the last hopes and possibilities for a successful school experience. That can be an awesome feeling. Conversely, when a student fails to make it in an alternative school, questions loom large about the source of the mismatch. Failure exists and it is our responsibility to learn from it on the road to mastering the art of alternative school teaching.

Yet another challenge for the alternative school teacher is the challenge to be healthy and fully functioning. The need to teach by example has never been more relevant than within an alternative education facility. We need to be there every day and model values supportive of the process. If we devalue the school or the process in any way, the students will attach themselves to that sentiment faster than to any concept we ever hoped they would grasp.

Everyone in the school needs to model appropriate behavior. It is not OK for students to experience a double standard. Staff and students are held to the same ethical and behavioral standards. Just as the smoky teachers' lounge has disappeared at the comprehensive high school, there is not a place for a dysfunctional staff member in an alternative education setting. "Why I can get stoned and you can't" is not valid for these chemically challenged and challenging students. This will be their first line of demarcation. Breaking through their resistance to decrease self-defeating behaviors will be one of the first tasks of the successful alternative school. Failing to address this issue will surely be the demise of the school as well.

The staff needs to reflect and respect the diversity of the school and the community that it serves. The best way to build trust with a student is to have an understanding of "where they are coming from." This ability to relate to the dilemmas that these students face is fundamental to their ability to develop a positive relationship with the teachers. Also, cultural comprehension increases the teacher's ability to relate to the issues of the family. The need for multicultural understanding and education among all members of the community are key to achieving harmony within the school as a whole (Wasserman, 1997).

Mentors and Mentorship

We who lived in concentration camps can remember the men who walked through the huts comforting others, giving away their last piece of bread. They may have been few in number, but they offer sufficient proof that everything can be taken from a man but one thing: the last of the human freedoms—to choose one's attitude in any given set of circumstances, to choose one's own way. (Frankl, 1963, p. 104)

The role of the staff at an alternative school closely parallels mentoring relationships. Because of the connection between mentoring attributes and the role of alternative education staff, a close examination of successful mentoring strategies is instructive.

Historic roots of the concepts underlying the mentor process may be as old as humankind itself. A mentor is any person with seniority or authority that can provide leadership to a younger protégé; a mentor may take many forms. In its simplest definition, mentorship is a helping relationship. The mentor could be a teacher, a caring adult, or an older student.

The quest for a mentor/hero to help ourselves emerge toward fulfillment or self-actualization (Maslow, 1968) was eloquently described by Joseph Campbell in *The Power of Myth* (1988). He describes our literature as being replete with hero legends dating as far back as ancient Greece, for example, the tales of Ulysses' epic journey. These stories recount the values inherent in relationships with the gods and the inspiration of their higher power. For our more earthly alternative education students, we must seek mentors/ leaders to provide some real-world examples of how they can be successful on their own journeys through life.

Since the evolution of our society to a postmodern period, we have seen significant changes that make the role of mentor important (Peters and Lankshear, 1996). The changes in family structure have left many children without the benefit of a biological parent, often the father (Markert, 1997). The cultural capital (Bourdieu, 1993; Giroux, 1996; McLaren, 1994) of knowledge—skills, language, manners, education, and experience—needs to be transferred by a significant other. In the absence of familial support, this social support could be given by a positive mentor. When a student has only negative support from adults who encourage criminal behavior or support dropping out of school (Duncan, 1994), a positive mentor might mitigate the negative influence of habitus (MacLeod, 1995).

The loss of traditional forms of leadership in our society has caused a recent surge of interest in the mentorship process (Darling, 1986). According to Darling (1986), "When mentor bonding occurs, the young person has natural access to the resources of the tribe" (p. 4).

The founding of the first youth mentor program began in 1904. In that year Ernest K. Coulter started the big brother movement (Grossman and Garry, 1997). This effort later became the Big Brothers/Big Sisters of America (BB/BS). Because of the effectiveness of BB/BS, mentoring methods have received recognition for their contributions to young people's success. For example, a recent study by Public/Private Ventures (P/PV) concluded, "...mentored youth were less likely to engage in drug or alcohol use, resort to violence, or skip school. In addition, mentored youth were more likely to improve their grades and their relationships with family and friends" (Grossman and Garry, 1997, p. 2).

The emerging prominence of mentoring has spawned an international conference and, concurrently, the formation of the International Association for Mentoring in 1986 (Darling, 1986).

Although much of the literature on mentoring is specifically written to address the needs of nurses (Bayles and Park-Doyle, 1995), new teachers (McIntyre and Hagger, 1988), or other new professionals (Wunsch, 1994), there is an emerging body of literature germane to the process of mentoring youth (Freedman and Jaffe, 1993; Springborn, 1997). Marie Wunsch, vice-chancellor for academic affairs at the University of Wisconsin, is a noted advocate for mentorship initiatives. She says, "Organizations really do benefit from mentoring programs. This truth should be fully acknowledged" (p. 12).

The literature of mentoring contains a wealth of information about what works. From the P/PV study, two major factors appear to be key to the success of mentors (Grossman and Garry, 1997). BB/BS require a commitment of four hours per week for three sessions per month. This length of time and the emphasis upon the mentor's friendly support appears to be the dominant factors in program success. Additional elements of structure that contribute to the program are: the screening out of potential problem mentors; training in communication skills; the matching of mentors with youth preferences; and intensive supervision by a case manager.

Much of the literature written to address the needs of at-risk youth mentions mentors as aides in the effort to assist youth in crime reduction, school success, and relationship development (Ingersoll and LeBoeuf, 1997). Citing a 1995 study by Rossman and Morley, Ingersoll and LeBoeuf state, "Every child needs and deserves a personal one-on-one relationship with a caring adult..." (p. 8).

The notion of mentorship has the greatest meaning and significance for at-risk youth. Because of the lack of other protective features in the lives of these youth, this personalization of the educational process needs to be high on the agenda of the alternative school. Having a small school and a commitment to all of the individuals in the school are the key contributing factors in the development of interpersonal trust and resiliency necessary to complete high school (Bates, Chung, and Chase, 1996).

Of the population at risk, minority, and especially African American, youth are at the very center. Dropout rates for African American youth hover near the fifty percent mark. The special needs of this cohort cry out even more for sensitive mentor relationships. To achieve honest and open dialogue with minority groups, mentors of like ethnicity are essential. In the necessary dialogue about racism, the literature points to the need for whites to take a back seat (Watson-Gegeo, Maldonado-Guzman, and Gleason, 1981). Interestingly, a group of British researchers found that they were able to obtain information that helped them understand the problems of minority Americans where American white researchers may have failed. For example, "Clem Adleman and Saville Kurshner, British researchers who have conducted a study of racial attitudes in a Black school in Boston over the past two years, report that they felt they had little problem gaining entry to the school because they are British. They argue that had they been American, access would have been difficult to gain because Blacks would have felt threatened by speaking openly about racism to Whites who they perceived as parties themselves to the racial conflict" (Watson-Gegeo, Maldonado-Guzman, and Gleason, 1981, pp. 15–16).

Unique in the world of mentoring is a program based in the San

Francisco Bay area called SportsBridge (Springborn, 1997). SportsBridge pairs female athletic mentors from Bay area colleges and the corporate world with middle grade girls. Attempting to capture the interest of girls during the dynamic period of adolescence, SportsBridge hopes to prevent drug abuse or other problems and support positive development.

Founded by Ann Kletz in 1995, SportsBridge appears to be gaining support. According to author Springborn, "Kletz stresses that sports is a vehicle for lifelong lessons. Through athletics these girls learn to compete, cooperate with one another, deal with success and failure, and maintain long-lasting relationships. They develop a heightened self-image, a greater self-confidence, and an increased awareness about healthy habits" (Springborn, 1997, p. 26).

The program Reading and Writing Across the Curriculum also offers a positive contribution by using college students and student athletes in the classroom to mentor academic success (Cavanaugh, 1997). Students from John Carroll University were paired with a group of nine- to twelve-year-old elementary school students in an after-school program to help their reading and writing skills. The college students first were trained in a course in reading and writing strategies for whole-group, small-group, and individual settings. After training, the college students and their mentees were matched at the school site. The tutorial program lasted approximately eight weeks. The results were positive. In the words of author Cavanaugh, "...The linking of college students with school children produces the kind of quality experiences and results that we want in our schools" (Cavanaugh, 1997, p. 55).

The spring 1997 issue of *Preventing School Failure* dedicated its focus to mentoring. Within the issue, the subject of mentoring received strong support (Guetzloe, 1997). It appears clear from the research that mentoring has the possibility to provide significant protective features for youth (Miller, 1997). This aspect of resiliency development may make for more successful youth.

Although mentoring has much to recommend it as an approach to reducing risk in youth, mentoring alone is not the answer to the problems of education or criminal justice (Rockwell, 1997). Mentoring needs to be a part of a comprehensive plan for school improvement. Hopefully, by forging stronger bonds between youth and adults we will be able to more strongly connect youth and school

(Townsel, 1997). Within the setting of the alternative school, those bonds are essential in order to link our students with successful school completion.

CHAPTER 13

Innovations in Summer School

Whether from an educational or therapeutic point of view, effective learning occurs in an environment where what is learned can immediately be put into practice. (Prouty, Radclif, and Schoel, 1988, p. 94)

After watching some of our students struggle with the credit-banking game that high school often becomes, the staff at the Alt school felt the need to develop a way for our students to earn a significant amount of credit in a short period of time. Our purpose was to accelerate several of our sixteen- and seventeen-year-old freshmen so that they could soon become juniors or seniors. The dilemma we were facing was that as our students were gaining maturity they were seeing themselves in relationship to the younger, fourteen-year-old ninth-graders sitting next to them in classes. This disparity was another alienating factor or impetus to drop out. In order for them to stay in school, they needed to have the hope that they would graduate relatively soon. To help achieve this miraculous eventuality, we created the alternative summer school.

Alternative summer school was designed to help students earn a semester's worth of credit in a three-week intensive program. The program consisted of a traveling school that was essentially an eighteen-hour per day class. Learning began at daybreak and continued until the last eye closed at night. Using this method of calculating "seat time," we were able to add significant credit hours to the records of our students.

Planning and all of the necessary preparations for the summer school took months. We began with fantasies of where our odyssey would take us. These discussions with the students built interest in the program. The talks also helped the students visualize themselves still in school while we continued our planning through the long New England winter. Finally, when summer came, we felt that we were ready to experience Alt summer school.

The first and biggest challenge was to dry out the students. Many of our students were heavy pot smokers and drinkers. To get them to calm down and believe that they could in fact live through some time without "partying," we spent our first four days on a sixty-four–acre island in the middle of a large estuary on the coast of Maine. The island had no stores or inhabitants. Owned by the Appalachian Mountain Club, Beal Island's peacefulness and serenity was an ideal place to detox our students and begin summer school.

Beal Island's best feature was its wonderful tidewater canoeing. We were able to paddle with the tide up into Monsweag Bay and observe ospreys, eagles, and sea birds of all varieties. When we returned, we took advantage of the tide change, and we were helped back to camp. There, the students cooked their own meals and generally kept the camp in order. At Beal Island we were able to establish routines that would serve us well for the next two-and-a-half weeks.

From the island, we headed north to the White Mountains. In the mountains, we had the opportunity to hike and enjoy the rivers in the warmth and beauty that summer brings to New Hampshire. Student learning there included mountain history and geology. Journals were the main method of recording observations and discoveries. Upon our return to the Alt, the journals became the core of an evaluation data.

The second half of our odyssey moved us out of New England. One evening right after dinner we left the small cabin we had rented and drove all night from the White Mountains to arrive at dawn the following morning in Hershey, Pennsylvania. In Hershey, we camped for several days of play in Hershey Park. The students loved the opportunity to play in the park and to tour the Hershey factory. I found Intercourse, Pennsylvania, to be of their liking, as well!

From Hershey, we drove to Washington, D.C. There we camped outside the city in a KOA campground and commuted on the Metro each day to tour the city. Our visits included the Smithsonian museums, Congress, Arlington National Cemetery, the Lincoln Memorial, and the National Gallery of Art. The Washington visit was rich with learning about politics, culture, and history.

The alternative summer school concluded with two days of classes back at the school. The purpose was to wrap up the trip and to produce a summary of the learning from our experiences. This debriefing was a very important aspect of the summer school. From the students, we were able to gauge the value of their experiences and to evaluate our effectiveness as teachers. We found the summer school to work well on many levels.

Through the student evaluations, we learned that the Alt summer school was very successful in achieving its goals of reducing drug and alcohol use among our students and in helping them to earn the credits they needed to move ahead in school. Both of those accomplishments were extremely significant. More than once during our trip, the students would comment that they hadn't played or had fun with their friends without using an illegal substance since they were in elementary school. That our students could see themselves in a happy state without chemical intervention was worth the work of the whole program!

The alternative summer school continued to evolve over the years. We stopped going to Washington because of the great driving distance. Our focus changed to New England. New England has boundless summer activities, and, in case of an emergency, we would always be within a few hours' drive from home.

In 1989, I left the alternative school to move to California. At that time a new team of teachers came to the alternative school to assume vacancies created by my move and the move of one of the other counselors. These changes meant two new staff hires and concomitant school climate adjustments. Unfortunately, the Alt was about to be rocked by a freakish event that no one could foresee.

The Wonalancet Alternative School was shaken with the Paulene Halyn incident and the ill effects of that incident plagued the school for years. For those readers unaware of the Paulene Halyn case, Mrs. Halyn, a staff member at the Wonalancet District Office, cunningly convinced three boys to assassinate her husband. She told the boys that her husband was physically and psychologically abusive. Using her strong persuasive skills, she further convinced the boys that by feigning to rob the apartment, her husband's assassination would never be suspected.

This incident and the subsequent trial rocked the community. It also challenged the Alt staff because of the divisions between the students aligned with Halyn and those opposed. The small community was torn by conflicting allegiances between families and neighbors. In the ensuing months, one of the Alt boys was beaten nearly to death for testifying against his "friends."

As the Halyn trial unfolded, the Alt school struggled under the new leadership. Divisions among staff members and conflicts between the staff and students led to a period of declining enrollment and the collapse of strong support from the school board and administration. As I received news of the events in New Hampshire in my new California home, I was frustrated to observe and hear of the struggles surrounding the Alt.

The events at that Alt reinforce the absolute value of staff in an alternative school. Staff make or break the school. The philosophy and the curriculum are of no value if they do not have credible and caring individuals to implement them. As staff, we hold a tremendous responsibility for the success and failure that our students experience. I do not believe that every at-risk kid is a good candidate for instruction or rehabilitation. There will always be a number of students that need to be removed for the safety of themselves or others. However, the vast majority of at-risk students are able to achieve success within the right program. Certainly program evaluators need to keep a watchful eye on student success as a means of gauging staff effectiveness.

I also believe that teachers are made, not born (Jelmberg, 1993). To this end, I think that the university could be of tremendous value as a resource to train and prepare teachers to work in alternative schools and other institutions that teach the students that have left either the public school or have been removed from society and are in need of rehabilitation education. Moreover, as educators are seeing greater numbers of at-risk students move through the regular education system, teachers and administrators at comprehensive school sites need to learn effective techniques for interacting with this population (Giroux, 1981). Giroux (1981) states the quintessence of the process. He says, "Teaching must be viewed...as a deeply personal affair" (p. 158).

Because the skills necessary to reach and teach these students are specific to psychology, counseling, and rehabilitation theory, a combination or multidisciplinary preparation program would help teacher education students and the institutions they will eventually serve. Teacher education needs to revamp its sequence of study to include courses in teaching disaffected youth with particular emphasis on critical pedagogy (Giroux, 1981). Without adequate teacher training, we will continue to lose students as teachers struggle to accommodate them using the inadequate and ineffectual practices that continue to perpetuate the values of the dominant culture.

Unfortunately, many good new teachers are lost to the profession through burnout because they harbor naive expectations about their jobs. To fill California's need for the 45,000 new teachers that are required within the next three years (by 2001), additional training in methods of dealing with disaffected youth could help prevent many students from failing and perpetuating the cycle of failures that can result in their leaving school or dismissal. By helping new teachers understand the dilemmas that many of their students face, a university training could help both students and teachers be more successful, and more fulfilled. Young teachers need to realize that all of our students are important, and that diversity is our strength.

Evaluation and Assessment

The purpose of education is to cultivate right relationship, not only between individuals, but also between the individual and society. (Krishnamurti, 1953, p. 34)

Critical to the success of both the staff and the students is a proven sense of accomplishment. To a greater degree than any other population, this community of learners needs to be able to clearly feel and see the products and outcomes of their efforts. This means clear goals and expectations. Students must expect that there is an interconnection between their education and future success in the areas of work, family, and community.

Evaluation in an alternative education setting directly relates to the material that is taught and is considered to be an integral part of the learning process. The purpose of assessment is to demonstrate competence and to further the instructional process. Therefore, testing is replaced by performance assessment. In performance assessment, student work is gathered in portfolios so the students may tangibly demonstrate what has been accomplished. In modern psychometric parlance, this is also known as authentic or alternate assessment. According to Posner (1995), "What makes [portfolios] authentic is the opportunity they afford for students to use their knowledge and skills in accomplishing a real world task" (p. 243).

Authentic assessment includes all the components that occur naturally within the school environment that are related to student output and behavior (Drummond, 1996). Examples of techniques relevant to an authentic assessment include interviews, observations, situational "tests," and portfolios. Of these techniques, portfolios offer one the most efficient and positive approaches to the measurement of student outcomes.

Portfolios are also popular with parents. Parents appreciate seeing specific examples of the growth that their son/daughter has made in class. The students, too, feel a sense of pride in the work that they've accomplished. Just as putting the work up on the wall for all to see can build pride, so can seeing the work gathered in a personally bound and decorated portfolio increase feelings of competency.

To help young people make the transition from antistudent to student, it is best to avoid traditional tests as a method of evaluating learning in alternative education settings. Not only do tests perpetuate bias, they also often only vaguely connect to learning as the purpose of the instruction. In the words of Reginald Jones (1988), "Even though we may develop tests and measures which are not racially or culturally discriminatory, they may not predict educationally meaningful performance or provide information that facilitates the development of instructional activities" (p. 23).

Often, the educational system's argument for testing is that the students need to learn how to take tests because they will be exposed to this later in their schooling. I contend that is not logical for alternative education students to become familiar with this process to prepare for future reintegration with the high school. If they go back, they may cope with the tests that regular education uses and accept those tests as a normal part of that system, or they may not. They do not need to take tests in an alternative education setting as a practice. Alternative school students need to change their attitude toward school in a present tense; tests do not facilitate any smooth transition nor do they contribute to the construction of positive relationships.

It is important to note that in alternative schools many of the students are second language learners. For this group, it is essential that alternative or authentic assessment techniques are used. Authentic assessment implies the use of authentic materials, or elements that serve a real purpose outside the classroom (Freeman and Freeman, 1994). This need to connect to a real-world experience is especially vital for second language learners because so few tests or other objective techniques have been normed for them. Therefore, the use of objective testing would yield invalid results (Estrin, 1993). Furthermore, because second language learners abound in alternative education settings and because alternative education students in general have similar literacy needs, authentic assessment is especially appropriate as a replacement for testing.

Making the student's school experience relevant should be the number one objective of everyone at the school. To establish personal meaningfulness or relevancy, goal-setting is critical to student success. Preparation for immediate future employment or for further study (for example, college) requires different high school strategies. A plan to implement the achievement of those goals gives the student a greater sense of purpose, fosters success, and provides hope. These goal-setting activities are well suited for the portfolio process.

Within the domain of assessment, students need the opportunity to evaluate teachers and to assist the teachers in their betterment as professionals. As university teachers are evaluated by their students, so should be the teachers of high school students (Bomotti, 1996). Because the factor of the relationship between the student and the teacher is so critical to the success of the alternative school student, this item bears constant scrutiny by all members of the school community. Certainly how the students perceive the teachers and the administrators needs to be given credibility.

Evaluation of the teachers connects with the evaluation of the school as a whole. These evaluations of the school need to be accomplished on a regular basis. The school needs imput from the community, parents, students, and staff members as a means of gauging the success of its programs. Conversely, the administration needs to be made aware of weaknesses in its programs in order to eliminate potentially dangerous or deleterious experiences.

The public opinion about the alternative school is key to its credibility with parents, students, and the community at large. It should be the goal of every alternative school to be the very best in its ability to analyze and serve the needs of its constituency. Having good communication with the superintendent and the school board should be a priority of the alternative school administration (Goodman, Fulbright, and Zimmerman, 1997). Surely, failing at this task will be the demise of the school.

An alternative school cannot succeed unless students are willing to come to the school and contribute to its success. The ability to gauge the strength and the effectiveness of the relationships that the alternative school is mandated to foster is the reason and purpose of the assessment process. Frequent reevaluations of the effectiveness of the school staff and their relationships with students will go a long way toward maintaining a high-quality, long-lasting alternative school.

Why Some School Districts Won't Change

In order to do the job it has undertaken and to find continuous public support for that, the criminal law organization must always keep alive a negative stereotype of the criminal. (Bianchi, 1994, p. 336)

Although there are many compelling arguments for the promotion of alternative schools, many school superintendents and the school boards that they represent feel that marginalized youth need punishment, not rehabilitation or a rewarding educational experience. Gauging from the nation's current penchant for building prisons, it appears that this thinking is more mainstream than this author would like to concede. Yet another view of why we do not have greater choice or alternative schools when the need for different types of educational processes is so apparent is eloquently expressed by Henry Giroux (1996), who states:

Rather than embracing cultural democracy, mainstream educators have largely embraced the modernist distaste for difference and fiercely promoted cultural uniformity as an aim of schooling. Wedded to the modernist infatuation with reason, mainstream educators have had little to say about the affective investments that mobilize student identities or how the mobilization of desire and the body is implicated in the pedagogical regulations of schooling. (p. 14)

Widespread evidence supports the conclusion that our society believes that a strong punitive response is the necessary reaction to antisocial behaviors (Braithwaite, 1989). Many educational leaders continue to advocate the swift removal of the miscreants and raising the bar of success through standards of excellence (Catterall and Moody, 1996; Orfield, 1988). This system fails to create alternative pathways to socialization and rehabilitation (Rotman, 1990). Without sufficient alternatives, how are we to reverse the growth of our prison populations and reduce the school's thirty-six percent attrition rate?

Gary Orfield (1988) has written extensively on the subject of the misapplication of standards of "excellence" in education. Because Blue Ribbon schools and Distinguished School awards are often the exclusive goal of today's educators, the excellence movement drives the goals to create bigger and better schools for successful students. Everyone can deduce that the betterment of our educational standards is for the greater good. However, the problem with those deductions is that this increase in standards is not designed to help those students in the lower quartiles of academics. This policy leaves to the low achievers the leftovers of the educational dinner plate because they become identified in some fashion as failures. The question then becomes, Whose standards? Who are the winners? According to Catterall and Moody (1996), "...increasing academic requirements in mathematics and social studies may perpetuate processes of disadvantage across groups of students in the secondary schools" (p. 160).

One of the biggest fallacies of educational thinking is to view meeting the needs of the disaffected as a "dumbing down" of the curriculum. The students who come to alternative school settings need basic skills. They also need social skills, pre-vocational skills, and self-help skills. For these students, this curriculum is not "dumb" nor does it make them less ready for society. The irony here is that it is the educators who reject alternative education who are ignorant. They fail to understand the needs of the growing constituency of at-risk learners, particularly in the context of today's multicultural and multidimensional communities.

Sadly, many administrators lack the ability to see the obvious connection between school success and societal success. The single largest factor that predicts future incarceration is the failure of a school system to prepare a student for societal success. When we do not develop new methodologies of instruction, we contribute to greater alienation from success for these very needy youth. Giroux (1996) remarks, "Education's slavish adherence to structuring the curriculum around the core disciplinary subjects is at odds with the field of cultural studies" (p. 17).

Unfortunately, the educational leaders and administrators are not the only ones who lack the tools to cope with these difficult students. The universities and teaching colleges have not been preparing teachers or administrators to work with these students. Without support and leadership from the universities, public schools will not be able to adequately staff the schools or educate the students that they are required to teach. The universities must take the lead in developing programs to train teachers for the vital and demanding role of teaching at-risk learners.

Collaborative efforts between local communities and nearby universities to develop programs to reach resistant learners will create opportunities to develop successful models of alternative education. Perhaps through further understanding of the methods of teaching the disaffected, resistance to providing alternative programs will lessen and more enlightened strategies will evolve.

The need to modernize teacher training is not limited to the needs of teachers of at-risk students. Because all children may possess some potential for risk factors, the new teacher preparation programs need to help all teachers see the value of psychologically inspired techniques. An example of the type of information that teachers of all children need to understand comes from Mick McManus's (1995) insightful study of at-risk youth. He states:

> A policy of understanding pupils has benefits for teachers but it also extends their professional responsibilities. Learning to analyze pupils' mental and emotional dispositions is necessarily learning to adopt a dispassionate and objective perspective. On learning of a pupil's fears we come to see behavior in a different light. Understanding provides partial insulation from personal involvement of a painful and overwhelming kind. Teachers can understand why they are the focus of the pupil's confused and misdirected feelings and not perceive such feelings as personal attacks. (p. 131)

As we begin the twenty-first century, we must increase our understanding of the diverse needs of our students and expand the alternatives available to them. If community residents do not come to understand the opportunity that alternative schools provide to young people that our society has previously failed, we will continue to see high rates of school attrition, and inevitably, growing rates of incarceration. I hope that as a society we can decrease our intellectual and moral polarization and come to see the expansion of alternatives in education as not only healthy, but sane.

What Doesn't Work

> Understanding school failure as the secondary effect of cultural
> capital and class- and gender-specific social practices runs directly
> counter to the prevailing neoconservative social logic, which attributes
> school failure to individual deficiencies on the part of a lazy, apathetic,
> and intellectually inferior underclass of students or to uncaring or
> selfish parents. (McLaren, 1994, p. 217)

It may seem absurd for me to talk about what doesn't work, but I
hope that my failures will help others learn as much as I did. Failures
can be as instructive as wins. Overall, the point of this chapter is that
we are human and mistakes are one of the things that we do! As
teacher-learners, we want to minimize our mistakes and, certainly,
not keep repeating them! When I reflect on some of my mistakes, I
can equate my most indelibly marked learning as a consequence of
self-inflicted poor judgment!

Mistake number one is to forget that failure hurts (Hill, 1991).
Although the fact is obvious, we continually need to remember this
truth. The students who come to the alternative school have failed in
regular education. They were, in most cases, thrown out. They often
have not elected to attend alternative school; they've been banished
there. In many cases, low self-esteem is well established by the time
an alternative education student comes to you. To ignore this is
denial. To continually disregard this truth is ignorance.

At the Alt school, we kept the knowledge of our difference alive
in many forms. Students were proud to have T. J. Rawlins as their
guest. The students strutted their defiance as an Alt attitude. These
affirmations meant that they were proud of the fact that they went to
the alternative school. "Nothing is more important than being
accepted and affirmed for who you are" (Hill, 1991, p. 310). Even the
alternative school motto: "Fuck that Shit," spoke to the students and
their own oppositional and defiant selves. The Alt students needed to
feel proud of who they were. It was a part of their continuing
struggle to find an acceptance of their uniqueness.

When we, as teachers, forgot to see our students as different from the students in the regular high school, we invariably found ourselves in situations that did not work. Alternative school students loathe tests. They have failed many times before, and they come to situations like testing ready for more failure. The word test is enough to throw them into a fit. Think of another way to get what you need in the way of evaluation other than using the testing strategy.

Eliciting confrontation is another example of poor choice on the part of the alternative school teacher. Confrontation is the last choice of a method to get a student to comply with a rule or even a request. Alternative education students are masters at confrontation, and the teacher is apt to lose a good number of times that they try this style. Threats of a detention often elicit, "Fuck that. Give me a suspension!" These students are used to being thrown out. That's familiar territory. They can then go home and smoke dope all day with no one to hassle them. Some consequence! That policy rewards bad behavior on both the part of the teacher and the student. The student doesn't have to come to school; the teacher doesn't have to face his/her failure to evoke an appropriate response because he or she used a methodology that handed out ineffectual punishments that were in fact rewards.

Another mistake is to call the parents to inform them that you *think* their kid may be using drugs. This bogus intervention can yield some interesting results! Remember the old cliché, "The family that prays together, stays together?" A modern equivalent may well be, "The family that gets high together, gets by together!" The film *The River's Edge* has several memorable scenes where the parents are yelling at the kids for stealing the last of their pot. Whereas that notion was phenomenal in years past, from the perspective of the Alt students watching the film, it was a typical irony of their family.

In an attempt to curtail one of my students from being constantly high, I made the mistake of calling mom at work and saying that I suspected her son was high all the time! About one hour later, a larger-than-life dad appeared in my office with a load of ire that scared the hell out of me! He demanded, "Why was I interfering in his family's private affairs?" All I could do was mutter meek, apologetic peeps in response. I'm fortunate to still be alive to tell the story!

If you believe drugs are the issue, take some time to find out where the family is on this issue rather than assuming that everyone agrees that drugs are bad. That could be a dangerous assumption. Calling the parent when you have no hard evidence of their student's use and confronting the parent's denial is not an intervention strategy. It is a set-up for failure with both the student and his or her family. You've clearly placed your relationship in an adversarial position. Recovering trust from a mistake like that one may be impossible.

Any imposition of our values onto the values of our students is a misuse of our power. Whether we are straight or gay, Democrat or Republican, born again or atheist, there is not a place for teachers to impose their values on the students in any school setting. Alternative education students need to find their own answers to the questions that they have. Our job is to guide them in their discovery of the truth and to help them make choices that will work for them. This is not to imply a valueless experience. We need to understand that diverse values represent the students and families that we serve. Helping our students make healthy and intelligent choices makes our job a vital and challenging one!

Effective Discipline Techniques

> I have argued that pupils' disruptive behavior may result from understandable perceptions, beliefs, and intentions; and that understanding and accepting this insulates the teacher from personal hurt, permits the possibility of communication and gains, however slowly, the pupils' attention and respect. (McManus, 1995, p. 130)

One of the most important components of a successful alternative school involves the discipline or behavior code. This code must reflect the unique characteristics of the community and students that the alternative school serves. Simply to copy the rules and regulations of the local high school will result in the same end product the high school achieved—a dropout. This does not mean that alternative school students have a carte blanche in the area of discipline. I would agree with Kellmayer (1995) that the alternative school should adopt the local high school rules regarding major safety violations. At a minimum, the community that the school serves needs to be assured that the students are safe (Carey, 1996). However, to disregard the unique needs of alternative school students and to treat them the same way as the traditional high school disregards essential differences and needs of these students.

In my work as a school psychologist and as an alternative educator, I have had the opportunity to witness hundreds of "misbehaviors" ranging from a simple "Fuck you" to more severe transgressions. One afternoon while driving back to school from an especially unsuccessful outing, the boys in the back of the Alt van were acting out their frustration with school, structure, and the world around them. As I occasionally gazed back at them from my driver's seat, I noticed the hostility growing. The day did not go their way, and I was going to have to pay for it in some way. As I glanced up once more in the rearview mirror, I saw a boy lunge at me with a knife. I ducked down in my seat and swerved the van to the side of the road. Laughter broke out in the back of the van. The boy, half smiling, said, "Only kidding!" For the next few nights, I awoke from sleep in a sweat thinking "What if that student's lunge with the knife was not a goof but was a real attempt to harm me? What if I had crashed the van?"

The learnings from such experiences, I am pleased to say, continue to provide me with stimulation and keep my work interesting! The vigilance required to work with at-risk youth because of their potential to exercise judgment of the poorest kind demands constant attention. This group also needs a strong set of rules to reinforce the need for the safety and respect of all of the participants.

Fundamental to the adoption of any rules or code of behavior is the tenet of mutual respect. As mentioned earlier, "No put-downs" is a good place to start. Similar to the Golden Rule in philosophy, the no put-down rule protects everyone from verbal and nonverbal abuse. Students are spared humiliation. Consistent with this rule, staff is expected to model respect for one another and the school that they serve. No one is devalued within the school community. This rule is key in the maintenance of the dignity and respect of all of the players within the school community. No exceptions!

No put-downs also means that the staff may not label the students as "bad." The students may be oppositional and defiant. They may resist conforming to the school rules. However, they are not to be devalued or labeled! Devaluing a student reinforces their disconnection with the school and rewards them with removal. The goal of an alternative education discipline code is to keep students in school, not to exclude them.

Developing an understanding of the student's misbehavior is fundamental if you want to keep the student in school (McManus, 1995). All behavior is purposeful and misbehavior is especially so. Whether the goal of the behavior is to avoid performing a task such as taking a test or to get the respect and admiration of a member of the opposite sex, the behavior has a subconscious or conscious motive.

Our task as educators is to maintain a detachment sufficient to stay in control and not get embroiled in the drama that unfolds. Humorist Joel Goodman likens the stance of the teacher to an Akido instructor. In the art of Akido, the individual recognizes the intent of a pugilist to engage them in a combat or a confrontation. The Akido master responds by getting out of the way of the blows of their opponent. The Akido master defeats the opponent by accepting the opponent's desire to hit them, but the master steps aside from each blow.

Educators need to see the misbehavior, but refuse to enter into conflict with the misbehavers. Like the two children endlessly saying, "Yes, you did"—"No, I didn't!" confronting negative behavior with direct assault perpetuates the interaction. Very often the student wins the reward of having the teacher or staff be his/her adversary, and the student gets to be a hero with his/her peers. The student fought the teacher, and the teacher succumbed to that level. Remember, with alternative education students, the punishment is often the reward! The irony of this fact is paralleled by the status a petty criminal receives when he (typically a male) matriculates from the county jail to a state penitentiary. Coming back to the "homies" in the neighborhood from the big house conveys status (Duff and Garland, 1994).

For many alternative education students, the misbehavior is rewarding in and of itself. Wilson (1983) notes, "Persons who are 'at risk' are those who lack strong, internalized inhibitions against misconduct, who value highly the excitement and thrills of breaking the law, who have a low stake in conformity, who are willing to take greater chances than the rest of us" (p. 188). When students have such motivations, alternative educators should not be surprised to see many kinds of misbehavior in the classroom. The trick is to avoid labeling and reinforcing the misbehavior (Braithwaite, 1989).

A way to mitigate the adolescent's innate desires to take risks and to be peer oriented is to accept those truths, to include the use of that knowledge in the establishment of program, and to develop bonds that will enhance the investment of students in their own education process. Control theory suggests that school, family, and milieu are the foundation of social bonding (Braithwaite, 1989).

Furthermore, Braithwaite (1989) states:

> There are four aspects of the social bond—attachment, commitment, involvement, and belief. Attachment means the emotional connection one feels toward other people, sensitivity to their opinions, feelings, and expectations. Commitment is the investment accumulated in relationships, the rational aspect of the social bond, the stake in conformity. Involvement refers simply to participation in legitimate activities—the extent to which the individual is tied to appointments, deadlines, working hours, plans.

Belief means acceptance of the desirability of obeying the rules of society. (p. 27)

These constructs need to be recognized as fundamental to the development of an alternative school discipline structure. If the students are bonded to the school and their friends, they will be less likely to vandalize school property or to engage in fights or other disruptive behavior. Control theory suggests the creation of harmonized relationships to mitigate opposition. For students available for relationships, this understanding of control theory is essential in the creation of a positive learning climate.

At the Wonalancet Alternative School, our best times were ones during which the social bonds were alive and circumscribed by an activity that everyone accepted. The best example was our traditional Thanksgiving dinner. At this event, all of our school came together and celebrated the holiday as a family. Students would discuss the event for weeks prior to the day. People would bring in their favorite dishes, and the atmosphere was cordial. The building of bonds that occurred with the sharing of celebration contributed greatly to the school staff's ability to reach the students on an emotional level.

When people outside of our school would come to visit, I would often point to our bathroom as a symbol of the students' true feelings about the Alt. The reason that I chose the bathroom as a symbol is that in schools the bathroom is one of the few places where students can go and have privacy. As a result, the bathroom is often adorned with gang writing, insults, and other text reserved for that location. Inside our unisex bathroom, we never had one word of graffiti! I interpreted this to be a sign of the respect that our students had for their school.

I am convinced that punishment is the wrong method for dealing with the misbehavior of alternative education students. Logical consequences and other therapeutically oriented methods build rapport and enhance relationships (Beck, Rush, Shaw, and Emery, 1979; Ellis and Harper, 1975). Certainly, any one alternative school will not be sufficient to meet the needs of all students and some students may be too psychologically involved to be available for social bonding. However, appropriate placement is still not punishment!

It is often hard, as a teacher, not to feel that the misbehavior of a student is an affront to oneself or the process that we as educators represent. However, it is essential that we not personalize and internalize the students' frustrations as attacks upon ourselves.

The need for a position of detachment was taken by Herbert Kohl (1969) twenty years earlier. "If the teacher considers defiance, disagreement, fights, or refusal to do a particular piece of work, to keep silent, or to line up, as a threat to authority, then a 'problem' is created" (p. 77). Giving respect and getting respect should be the essence of an alternative educator's discipline doctrine and that respect can become the gateway for social bonding. Failure to develop this fundamental tenet of resiliency will preclude the demise of the school. Only within a context of trust and mutual respect will alternative school students succeed.

CHAPTER 18

Uniqueness and Individuation

A million zeros joined together do not, unfortunately, add up to one. Ultimately everything depends on the quality of the individual, but the fatally shortsighted habit of our age is to think only in terms of large numbers and mass organizations. (Jung, 1958, p. 67)

Although much of this book and the literature reviewed for its writing point to the need to systematize the processes of alternative school development (Pianta and Walsh, 1996), it is wrong to assume that the development of local alternative schools is other than a unique and individual process. Despite the success of nationally recognized programs such as Project Adventure or the School Development Project (SDP), the replication of these programs will be carried out by individuals other than Karl Rohnke or Dr. Comer. Even in the case of Jaime Escalanté, America's greatest teacher of *Stand and Deliver* fame, Mr. Escalanté was unable to repeat his Los Angeles success within the Sacramento schools (Matthews, 1989). This failure to replicate success was not that Mr. Escalanté had changed. The failure is related to a change of administration. The new administration was fundamentally unsupportive of Mr. Escalanté's idiosyncratic style (Matthews, 1989).

We have learned much from the models of success. It has been proven that we can successfully apply modern educational and psychological theory to make individual schools work. In inner-city New Haven, Dr. Comer's SDP has shown the nation a model of great worth and the SDP model has been successfully duplicated in many communities. However, without the knowledge, effort, determination, and will of individual educators, the changes would not have occurred (Senge, 1990). We know how to make individual schools successful. We cannot make the whole system work.

I am suggesting that to achieve greater rates of success we first need to focus on the individual schools and micromanage for success. It is my hope then that entire school systems and the large communities that comprise them will experience more successful schools from the sum of their parts.

My favorite example of micromanagement dates back thirty years. When I attended the Colorado Outward Bound School in the Summer of 1970, my instructor, Howie Hoffman, said something relevant and unforgettable. Standing on the edge of the Rocky Mountains for the beginning of my twenty-six-day experience, Howie told all eight of his charges that from this point on all of the literature and philosophy of Outward Bound was only a set of ideals. What we had ahead was a personal encounter with nature, Howie, and ourselves. That personal experience would become what Outward Bound was to be for us. True to Howie's words, my memory of Outward Bound has been a memory of those vivid experiences we shared as a group, far from the Outward Bound corporate offices.

As that experience was true for me, so is the experience of each and every individual student and family that experiences you, the teacher, or you, the educator, on a daily basis. The manuals are closed. The rhetoric and pedagogy is only a backdrop to the drama that unfolds daily for those individuals with whom we try to connect. Nothing could be more personally meaningful than those encounters. Unfortunately, in many communities across our country, we are closing entire schools because they have lost their connection to meaning and purpose of education.

The difference between success and failure rests within those individuals who show up every day and make their classrooms and schools work. These individuals manage the internal workings of their schools with craft. They know the diversity of their surroundings, and they celebrate the value of their constituents.

Supporting these educators are the individual communities and school boards that recognize that the contributions of alternative education are worth their investment. These communities realize that the costs of supporting an educational opportunity for all is much less costly than the expense of exclusion. These communities know that the costs of school failure are not only economic. The losses are aesthetic, cultural, environmental, and, most importantly, deeply personal. When a community loses people that might have been productive members of society, it indicates more than simply a demographic trend. Those people *are* our communities!

For these reasons, individual neighborhood initiatives are essential to the success of local alternative schools. No two communities are alike. According to Posner (1995), "Different situations require different practices" (p. 4). As we borrow from the literature to give birth to our own models, we need to continue to build upon our individual and community values to make our own way in this complex and confusing world. Change in the schools is a difficult and complex task (Sarason, 1990). When we take the first steps to define ideal schools for our youth, the students will sense our appreciation of them and, hopefully, learn how to continue that nurturing and learning process for the generations in our future.

As agents of change, we must also be wary of constituencies that may want to use alternative education initiatives as a way of removing miscreants from close proximity to the more affluent members of the community. Many communities that have been recognized with outward symbols of free choice such as vouchers would actually prefer to see disaffected students drawn away into magnet schools that segregate such students from comprehensive high schools. This method of exploitation of the alternative education process is not democratic.

Many communities are buying the notion that schools need to be run by commercial enterprises unencumbered by the institutional need to adhere to democratic values. Rather than thinking of the community as a whole, profit and other capitalistic motivations replace the desire to help *all* students succeed. This motivation for increasing test scores and improving the "products" of education works to discriminate against students who lack the intelligence or aptitudes for success. This materialistic motivation underacknow-ledges the economically and culturally distinct populations that have traditionally been underrepresented. Looking at individuals as units or objects for education continues exclusionary practice. This com-modification of education contributes to covert racism. Research substantiates the increased exclusion that results from the "noble" cause of strategies to achieve "excellence" (Catterall and Moody, 1996; Orfield, 1988).

Educators who promote choice and the continuing development of alternative teaching methodologies must protect against being co-opted by those who would turn the alternative school into another mutation of either racist or economically exclusionary education. This caveat must be heeded or the alternative school can be sold out from its start. When the students arrive in their new alternative school and see that they all come from the same underrepresented neighborhood and share the same sense of alienation from the middle-class comprehensive school, you will never get beyond survival status as a school, and the lofty goals you dream of will never meet reality!

To avoid selling out to those who advocate exclusion, the developers of alternative programs need to involve the entire community in efforts to include students who need alternative methods of instruction. My experience at the Wonalancet Alternative School showed that all classes of students benefited from the difference in instruction. The broad base of community support validated the experience of everyone. True to our no put-down rule, no students were devalued for attending the Alt. No students who attend a democratically constructed alternative school should be devalued for their attendance. Educators show respect for students when they include multicultural values as part of their outreach efforts to parents and community members; consequently, students understand their teachers truly value their participation in the school.

We have far to go to reach goals of democratization of our schools and our other public institutions. However, by affirming our diversity and expanding the models of instruction that work, alternatives in education may work to ameliorate some of our school's failures and to generate a just and promising future for all of our citizens.

REFERENCES

Alper, L., D. Fendel, S. Fraser, and D. Resek. (1996, May). Problem-based mathematics—Not just for the college bound. *Educational Leadership* 53 (8): 18–21.

Altenbaugh, Richard J., David E. Engel, and Don T. Martin. (1995). *Caring for students: a critical study of urban school leavers*. Bishop, Pa.: The Falmer Press.

Apple, Michael W. (1995). *Education and power*. New York: Routledge.

Applebome, Peter. (1997). Dispute over Ebonics reflects a volatile mix that roils urban education. *The New York Times*, March, p. 8.

Baker, Jean A., Robert Bridger, Tara Terry, and Anne Winsor. (1997). Schools as caring communities: A relational approach to school reform. *School Psychology Review* 26 (Fall): 586–602.

Bates, M., A. Chung, and M. Chase. (1996). Where has the trust gone? *CASP Today* (Summer): 14–15.

Bayles, Patricia and Jodi Parks-Doyle. (1995). *The web of inclusion: Faculty helping faculty*. New York: National League of Nursing.

Beck, Aaron T., John A. Rush, Brian F. Shaw, and Gary Emery. (1979). *Cognitive therapy of depression*. New York: The Guilford Press.

Benard, Bonnie. (1991). *Fostering resiliency in kids: Protective factors in the family, school and community*. Portland: Northwest Regional Educational Laboratory.

Bianchi, Herman. (1994). Abolition: Assensus and sanctuary. In *A reader on punishment*, edited by Anthony Duff and David Garland. Oxford: Oxford University Press.

Bierlein, Louann A., and Lori A. Mulholland. (1994). The promise of charter schools. *Educational Leadership* 1 (September): 34–36.

Billings, Judith A. (1995). *Educational options and alternatives in Washington State*. Olympia, Wash.: Office of Superintendent of Public Instruction.

Bomotti, Sally. (1996). Why do parents choose alternative schools? *Educational Leadership* (October): 30–32.

Bourdieu, Pierre. (1993). *The field of cultural reproduction*. New York: Columbia University Press.

———. (1977). Cultural reproduction and social reproduction. In *Power and Ideology*, edited by J. Karabel and A. H. Halsey. New York: Oxford University Press.

Braithwaite, John. (1989). *Crime, shame, and reintegration.* Cambridge: Cambridge University Press.

Brockelman, Paul. (1985). *Time and self: Phenomenological explorations.* New York: Crossroad Publishing Company.

Bruner, Jerome S. (1966). *Toward a theory of instruction.* New York: W. W. Norton.

Cairns, Robert B. and Beverly D. Cairns. (1994). *Lifelines and risks: Pathways of youth in our time.* Cambridge, England: Cambridge University Press.

Campbell, Joseph. (1988). *The power of myth.* New York: Doubleday.

Canadian Cataloguing in Publication Data. (1994–95). *British Columbia. Ministry of education annual report.* (ISSN 1192–9545). Victoria, British Columbia: Ministry of Education.

Carey, Karen. (1996). Competent kids in safe schools. *NASP Communiqué* (Fall): 12.

Catterall, James S. and David E. Moody. (1997). Where excellence and preparedness meet: Increased course requirements and at-risk students. *The High School Journal* (December/January): 139–161.

Cavanaugh, Mary P. (1997). Learning from the big kids. *Educational Leadership* (April): 53–55.

Chalker, Christopher Scott. (1996). *Effective alternative education programs: Best practices from planning through evaluating.* Lancaster, Pa.: Technomic.

Comer, James P. (1988). Effective schools: Why they rarely exist for at-risk elementary school and adolescent students. *School success for students at risk: Analysis and recommendations of the council of chief state school officers.* Orlando, Fla.: Harcourt, Brace, Jovanovich, Inc.

———. (1980). *School power: Implications of an intervention project.* New York: The Free Press.

Coxford, Arthur F. and Christian R. Hirsch. (1996). A common core of math for all. *Educational Leadership* 53(8) (May): 22–25.

Cummins, Jim and Dennis Sayers. (1995). *Brave new schools: Challenging cultural literacy.* New York: St. Martin's Press.

Darling, Lu Ann W. (1986). In *Mentoring: Aid to excellence in career development, business, and the professions,* edited by William A. Gray and Marilyne Miles Gray. Vancouver, British Columbia: International Association for Mentoring.

103

DeVillar, Robert A. (1994). In *Cultural diversity in schools: From rhetoric to practice*, edited by Robert A. DeVillar, Christian J. Faltis, and James P. Cummins. Albany: State University of New York Press.

Dewey, John. (1916). *Democracy and education*. Toronto: MacMillan Co.

Drummond, Robert J. (1996). *Appraisal procedures for counselors and helping professionals*. Englewood Cliffs, New Jersey: Merrill.

Duff, Anthony and David Garland. (Eds.) (1994). *A reader on punishment*. Oxford: Oxford University Press.

Duncan, Greg J. (1994). Families and neighbors as sources of disadvantage in the schooling decisions of white and black adolescents. *American Journal of Education* 103 (November): 21–53.

Edwards, Willie J. (1996). A measurement of delinquency differences between a delinquent and non-delinquent sample: What are the implications? *Adolescence* 31 (Winter): 973–986.

Eggebrecht, J., R. Dagenais, D. Dosch, N. Merczak, M. Park, S. Styer, and D. Workman. (1996). Reconnecting the sciences. *Educational Leadership* 53 (8): 4–8.

Ellis, Albert and Robert A. Harper. (1975). *A new guide to rational living*. North Hollywood, Calif.: Wilshire Book Company.

Estrin, Elise Trumbull. (1993). Alternative assessment: Issues in language, culture, and equity. In *Knowledge Brief* (11). San Francisco: Far West Laboratory.

Fontana, Cyndee and Draeger Martinez. (1997). Taking control of our children. *The Fresno Bee*, 23 March, p. B9.

Frankl, Victor. (1963). *Man's search for meaning*. New York: Washington Square Editions.

Freedman, Marc and Natalie Jaffe. (1993). Elder mentors: Giving schools a hand. *National Association of Secondary School Principals Bulletin* (January): 22–28.

Freeman, David E. and Yvonne S. Freeman. (1994). *Between worlds: Access to second language acquisition*. Portsmouth, New Hampshire: Heineman.

Furillo, Andy. (1995). What to do with troubled youth: Many daunting problems await CYA's next leader. *The Sacramento Bee*, 1 August, p. B1.

Gaines, Jack. (1979). *Fritz Perls: Here and now*. Tiburon, Calif.: Integrated Press.

Gass, Michael. (1993). *Adventure therapy: Therapeutic applications of adventure programming.* Dubuque, Iowa: Kendall Hunt.

Giroux, Henry A. (1996). *Fugitive cultures: Race, violence, and youth.* New York: Routledge.

————. (1983). *Theory and resistance in education: A pedagogy for the opposition.* South Hadley, Mass.: Bergin and Garvey Publishers, Inc.

————. (1981). *Ideology, culture, and the process of schooling.* Philadelphia, Pa.: Temple University Press.

Giroux, Henry A. and Peter McLaren. (1989). *Critical pedagogy, the state, and cultural struggle.* Albany, New York: State University of New York Press.

Giroux, Henry, Colin Lankshear, Peter McLaren, and Michael Peters. (1996). *Counternarratives: Cultural studies and critical pedagogies in postmodern spaces.* New York: Routledge.

Goodman, Richard H., Luann Fulbright, and William G. Zimmerman. (1997). *Getting there from here: School board-superintendent collaboration: Creating a school governance team capable of raising student achievement.* Arlington, Va.: Educational Research Service.

Grossman, Jean Baldwin and Eileen M. Garry. (1997). Mentoring—A proven delinquency prevention strategy. *Juvenile Justice Bulletin* 52 (April 1997): 1–7.

Guetzloe, Eleanor. (1997). The power of positive relationships: Mentoring programs in the school and community. *Preventing School Failure* (Spring): 100–104.

Harris, Thomas A. (1969). *I'm okay—you're okay.* New York: Harper & Row.

Hart, Leslie A. (1983). *Human brain and human learning.* Oak Creek, Ariz.: Books for Educators.

Haynes, N. M. and J. P. Comer. (1996). Integrating schools, families, and communities through successful school reform: The school development program. *School Psychology Review* 25 (4): 501–506.

Hill, Don. (1991). Tasting failure: Thoughts of an at risk learner. *Phi Delta Kappa* (December): 308–310.

Hillman, James. (1996). *One hundred years of psychotherapy: And the world is getting worse.* New York: Random House.

Hirsch, E. D., Joseph F. Kett, James Trefil. (1991). *The dictionary of cultural literacy: What every American needs to know.* Boston:

Houghton Mifflin.

Hunt, Morton. (1993). *The story of psychology.* New York: Doubleday.

Ingersoll, Sarah and Donni LeBoeuf. (1997). Reaching out to youth out of the educational mainstream. *Juvenile Justice Bulletin* (February 1997): 1–11.

Jelmberg, J. R. (1993). Alternative certification in New Hampshire: Perceptions of teachers and principals. Ph.D. diss., University of New Hampshire.

Jeub, Chris. (1995). Why parents choose home schooling. *Educational Leadership I* (September): 50–52.

Jones, Reginald L. (1988). *Psychological assessment of minority group children.* Berkeley: Cobb and Henry Publishers.

Jung, C. G. (1958). *The undiscovered self.* New York: Mentor.

Kellmayer, John. (1995). *How to establish an alternative school.* Thousand Oaks, Calif.: Corwin Press.

Kohl, Herbert. (1969). *The open classroom.* New York: Vintage Books.

———. (1994). *I won't learn from you and other thoughts on creative maladjustment.* New York: The New Press.

Kopp, Sheldon. (1989). *Rock paper scissors.* Minneapolis, Minn.: CompCare Publishers.

Kozol, Jonathan. (1982). *Alternative schools.* New York: Continuum Press.

Krishnamurti, J. (1953). *Education and the significance of life.* New York: Harper & Row.

Lieberman, Lawrence M. (1986). *Special educator's guide to regular education.* Newtonville, Mass.: GloWorm Publications.

Luegers, S. (1997). Experiential education: Learning by doing. *Paradigm* (Summer): 14–15.

MacLeod, Jay. (1995). *Ain't no makin' it.* Boulder, Colo.: Westview Press.

Mahal, Taj. (1969). You don't miss your water ('til your well runs dry). On *The natch'l blues* [Record]. New York: Columbia.

Markert, Louis. (1997). Why fathers are such a big deal to their children. *The Fresno Bee,* 14 June, p. B7.

Maslow, Abraham H. (1968). *Toward a psychology of being.* New York: Van Nostrand Reinhold Company.

Matthews, Jay. (1989). *Escalenté: The best teacher in America.* New York: Henry Holt.

McCall, Nathan. (1994). *Makes me wanna holler.* New York: Vintage

Books.

McIntyre, Donald and Hazel Hagger. (1988). *Mentors in schools: Developing the profession of teaching.* London: David Fulton.

McLaren, Peter. (1994). *Life in schools: An introduction to critical pedagogy in the foundations of education.* New York: Longman Publishing.

———. (1997). *Revolutionary multiculturalism: Pedagogies of dissent for the new millennium.* Boulder, Colo.: Westview Press.

———. (1986). *Schooling as a ritual performance.* New York: Routledge and Kegan Paul.

McManus, Mick. (1995). *Troublesome behavior in the classroom.* London: Routledge.

Miller, Darcy. (1997). Mentoring structures: Building a protective community. *Preventing School Failure* (Spring): 105–109.

Moore, Thomas. (1992). *Care of the soul: A guide for cultivating depth and sacredness in everyday life.* New York: HarperCollins.

Moote, Gerald T. and John S. Wodnarski. (1997). The acquisition of life skills through adventure-based activities and programs: A review of the literature. *Adolescence* 32 (125): 143–167.

Munitz, Barry. (1995). *Never make predictions, particularly about the future.* Washington, D.C.: American Association of State Colleges and Universities.

National Association of Secondary School Principals. (1996). *Breaking ranks: Changing an American institution.* Reston, Va.: Commission on the Restructuring of the American High School.

National Commission on Excellence in Education. (1983). *A nation at risk: the imperative for educational reform.* Washington, D.C.: U.S. Government Printing Office.

Nieto, Sonia. (1996). *Affirming diversity: The sociopolitical context of multicultural education.* White Plains, N.Y.: Longman Publishers.

Ogbu, John U. (1995). Literacy and black Americans: Comparative perspectives. In *Literacy among African-American youth,* edited by V. L. Gadsden and D. A. Wagner. Cresskill, N.J.: Hampton Press, Inc.

Orfield, Gary. (1988). Race, income, and education inequality. In *School success for students at risk: Analysis and recommendations of the Council of Chief State School Officers.* Orlando, Fla.: Harcourt, Brace, Jovanovich, Inc.

Page, Clarence. (1996). *Showing my color: Impolite essays on race and identity*. New York: Harper Collins.

Page, Randy. (1996). Youth suicidal behavior: Completions, attempts, and ideations. *High School Journal* (October/November): 60–65.

Peng, Samuel S. (1994). Understanding resilient students: The use of national longitudinal databases. In *Educational resilience in inner-city America*, edited by Margaret C. Wang and Edmund W. Gordon. Hillside, N.J.: Erlbaum.

Peters, Michael and Colin Lankshear. (1996). Postmodern counter-narratives. In *Counternarratives: Cultural studies and critical pedagogies in postmodern spaces*, edited by H. Giroux, C. Lankshear, P. McLaren, and M. Peters. New York: Routledge.

Pianta, Robert C. and Daniel J. Walsh. (1996). *High-risk children in schools*. New York: Routledge.

Posner, George J. (1995). *Analyzing the curriculum*. New York: McGraw-Hill.

Prouty, D., P. Radcliff, and J. Schoel. (1988). *Islands of healing*. Hamilton, Mass.: Project Adventure, Inc.

Raywid, Mary Anne. (1995). Alternative schools: The state of the art. *Educational Leadership* I (September): 26–31.

Reif, Linda. (1984). Writing and rappelling. *Learning Magazine* 13 (September): 73–76.

Rockwell, Sylvia. (1997). Mentoring through assessable, authentic opportunities. *Preventing School Failure* 14 (Spring): 111–114.

Rogers, C. (1969). *Freedom to learn*. Columbus, Ohio: Charles E. Merrill Publishing Co.

Rohnke, Karl. (1981). *High profile*. Hamilton, Mass.: Project Adventure Press.

Rotman, E. (1990). Beyond punishment. In *A reader on punishment*, edited by Anthony Duff and David Garland. New York: Oxford University Press.

Sarason, Seymour B. (1990). *The predictable failure of school reform: Can we change course before it's too late?* San Francisco, Calif.: Josey-Bass.

Sawicky, Max B. (1997). Business-run schools: A leap of faith. *The Education Digest* (April): 29–33.

Senge, Peter M. (1990). *The fifth discipline: The art and practice of the learning organization*. New York: Doubleday.

Smith, Frank. (1978). *Reading without nonsense*. New York: Teachers College.

Soriano, M., G. Hong, and P. Mercado. (1996). School psychology and family services: Meeting the challenges in California's 21st century. *The California School Psychologist* 1 (May): 37.

Springborn, Beatrice. (1997). A model for success. *Woman's Sports and Fitness* (May): 26.

Taxel, Joel. (1989). Children's literature as an ideological text. In *Critical pedagogy, the state, and cultural struggle*, edited by Henry Giroux and Peter McLaren. Albany: State University of New York Press.

Teale, E. W. (Ed.) (1954). *The wilderness world of John Muir*. Boston: Houghton Mifflin Company.

Thompson, R. (1990). *Suicide and sudden loss: Crisis management in the schools*. (Report No.315–700). Ann Arbor, Mich.: National Center for Research on Counseling and Student Services. (ERIC Document Reproduction Service No. ED 315 700.)

Townsel, Kim T. (1997). Mentoring African-American youth. *Preventing School Failure* (Spring): 125–127.

Vigil, James Diego. (1988). *Bario gangs: Street life and identity in southern California*. Austin: University of Texas Press.

Wang, Margaret C., Geneva D. Haertel, and Herbert J. Walberg. (1994). Educational resilience in inner cities. In *Educational resilience in inner-city America*, edited by M. C. Wang and E. W. Gordon. Hillsdale, N.J.: Erlbaum.

Washington State Department of Education. (1995–96). *Educational options and alternatives in Washington State*. State Superintendent of Public Instruction Publication No. ES/016/95. Olympia, Wash.: Washington State Department of Education.

Wasserman, Jim. (1997). Arrogance, racism fly in the face of sanity. *The Fresno Bee*, 23 March, p. B1.

Watkins, Cheryl. (1992). *Student assistance program training*. Phoenix, Ariz.: Chemical Awareness Training Institute.

Watson-Gegeo, Karen A., Abdil A. Maldanado-Guzman, and John J. Gleason. (1981). Establishing research goals: The ethnographer-practitioner dialectic. In *Proceedings of Selected Research Paper Presentations, Theory, and Research Division*. Philadelphia, Pa.: Association for Educational Communications and Technology.

Wedge, Robert F. (1995). *California juvenile camps and ranches population*. Summary Report No. 17. Sacramento, Calif.: California Department of the Youth Authority Research

Division.

———. (1994). *California juvenile hall population*. Summary Report No. 25. Sacramento, Calif.: California Department of the Youth Authority Research Division.

Wilson, J. Q. (1983). Penalties and opportunities. In *A reader on punishment*, edited by Anthony Duff and David Garland. Oxford: Oxford University Press.

Wink, Joan. (1997). *Critical pedagogy: Notes from the real world*. New York: Longman.

Wirt, Fredrick M. and Michael W. Kirst. (1992). *Schools in conflict*. Berkeley: McCutchan Publishing Company.

Wunsch, Marie A. (Ed.) (1994). *Mentoring revisited: Making an impact on individuals and institutions*. San Francisco, Calif.: Jossey-Bass.

Young, Timothy W. (1990). *Public alternative schools: Options and choice for today's schools*. New York: Teachers College.

Zimmerman, Joy. (1994). Resiliency versus risk: Helping students help themselves. *Far West Focus* (May): 3.

INDEX